Death *in the* Grizzly Maze

Death *in the* Grizzly Maze

The Timothy Treadwell Story

Mike Lapinski

FALCON®

GUILFORD, CONNECTICUT
HELENA, MONTANA

AN IMPRINT OF THE GLOBE PEQUOT PRESS

This book is dedicated
to the memory of
Amie Huguenard
and
Timothy Treadwell

Text design: Tom Goddard
Cover photo credits: Front cover and back top left images by Ross Johnson, ©2004; back cover middle and top right images by Phil Schofield, ©1995 Phil Schofield, philschophoto@comcast.net
Maps by Robert Lindquist, Bob's Mapping Service with contributions by Stephen Stringall © The Globe Pequot Press

Library of Congress Cataloging-in-Publication Data
Lapinski, Michael.
    Death in the grizzly maze: the Timothy Treadwell story / Mike Lapinski.—1st ed. p. cm.
    ISBN 0-7627-3677-1
1. Bear attacks—Alaska—Katmai National Park and Preserve—Anecdotes. 2. Treadwell, Timothy, 1961- 3. Grizzly bear—Behavior—Alaska—Katmai National Park and Preserve. 4. Katmai National Park and Preserve (Alaska) I. Title.
    QL737.C27L339 2005
    599.784'092—dc22   2005042513

Manufactured in the United States of America
First Edition/First Printing

CONTENTS

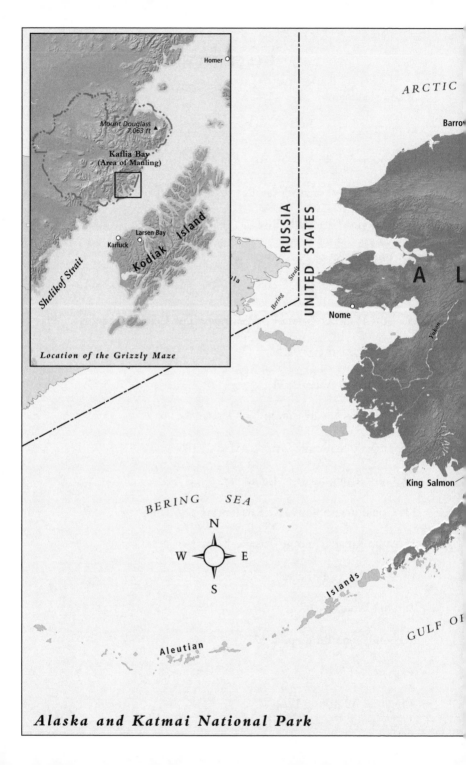

ARCTIC

Barrow

RUSSIA

UNITED STATES

Homer

Mount Douglass
7,063 ft

Kaflia Bay
(Area of Mauling)

Shelikof Strait

Larsen Bay
Karluck

Kodiak Island

Location of the Grizzly Maze

Bering Strait

A L

Nome

King Salmon

Yukon

BERING   SEA

N
W   E
S

Islands

Aleutian

GULF OF

Alaska and Katmai National Park

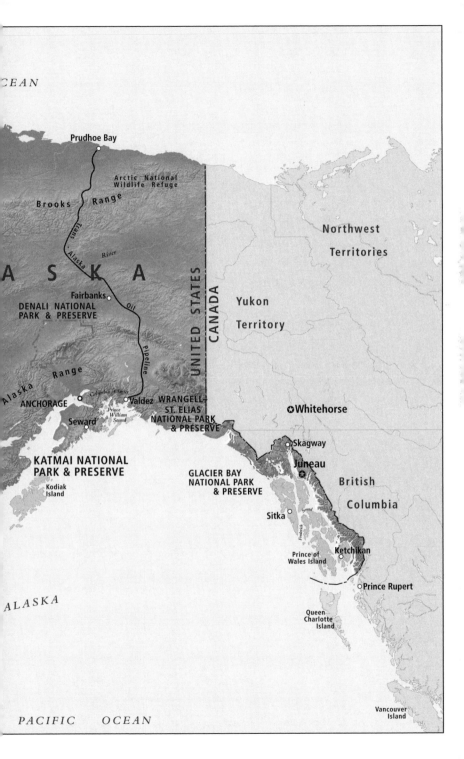

ACKNOWLEDGMENTS

This book would not have been possible without the encouragement and help of Chuck Bartlebaugh, Director of the Center for Wildlife Information, and the shared insights and expertise of biologists Tom Smith, Sterling Miller, Chuck Jonkel, and Stephen Stringham. My friend Mark Matheny also shared valuable opinions concerning bear pepper spray, and Roland Dixon was helpful and courageous in sharing his insights into the private life of Timothy Treadwell. I would also like to thank the family members and friends who spoke with me about Timothy and Amie, and gratefully acknowledge the time they gave me in their grief. Thanks also to the staff at Katmai National Park for their courteous treatment and prompt attention to my queries, and to former Katmai Park superintendent Deb Liggett for sharing her story. None of these people, however, are responsible for any omissions or errors I made during the course of this book.

A special thanks goes to editors Stephanie Hester and Erin Turner, who identified the need for this book and acted upon it, and to Mimi Egan for her editorial expertise in the making of this book.

Prologue

A COLD AUTUMN RAIN PELTS a small blue tent, and an occasional gust of wind sends the nylon fabric rippling in a series of loud snaps. It's early afternoon in Alaska's Katmai National Park. The sky is overcast; the light is gray.

On a nearby trail a young grizzly bear stops and raises his head, listening. Nothing. Then he hears it, the soft shuffling sound that has been coming from the trail behind him for the past half hour.

A branch cracks and the young bear spots movement. A big red bear is moving forward along the same trail. It's the same bear that attacked him earlier in the stream below.

The young bear bolts ahead, scrambling desperately through a tunnel in the dense underbrush. He runs for a hundred yards and stops at the edge of a small clearing.

The bear is tired and his injured shoulder aches. He licks at a seep of blood coming from the gash inflicted by the big red bear. More branches rustle behind him, and he jumps forward into the clearing. He lets out a startled "Huff!" when he sees the blue tent just 20 feet away.

The bear hears sounds coming from inside the tent; from behind him comes the sound of brush being shoved aside. The big red bear that slashed him earlier is still back there—following him. The young bear bounds forward, pounding his paws on the ground, growling and popping his jaw.

A sharp, threatening sound comes from the tent. The young bear jumps back and starts to turn away, but the terrifying noise of the big red bear's labored breathing as it trudges up the hill sends him back the other way. A half-bawl, half-frightened roar blasts from the young bear's throat.

A man zips open the tent door and steps gingerly outside onto the cold, wet grass. At first he sees nothing. Then he smells it—the powerful odor of rotting fish that bears can give off. He turns to his right and spots the young bear, now just 15 feet away from the tent. It's a young bear, though there's fear in its eyes.

The man rises to his full height and spreads his arms to look bigger. He takes a few quick steps toward the bear and begins to yell, making a loud noise.

The bear lunges, and the man instinctively spins away. But the blow catches the man on the shoulder and sends him sprawling. And then the bear is on him, ripping and tearing at him with its jaws.

A cry comes from the tent, but the only reply is a strangled grunt amid the violent swishing of alders and the thud of a body hitting the ground. There's a loud shriek, then another scream.

A woman steps out of the tent; she gasps when she sees the man lying on his back, a bear biting at his arms and hands as he fights it. There is blood all over the man's head and arms, and the woman begins to wail. The young bear rears back. For a long moment the only sound is the falling rain. The man struggles to rise, and the bear pounces on him again, tearing at his shoulder and shaking him violently.

Shock sends the woman stumbling back against the tent, screaming and wailing as she watches the horrific scene before her.

The bear moves away from the bloody body on the ground and turns toward the woman, swiping at her with one of its heavy, claw-tipped paws . . .

The big red bear smells blood before he reaches the opening. The young bear hears the oncoming brute and scampers away. The big red bear lumbers into the clearing. He moves forward toward the bodies. He drags the first body down a trail and feeds on it, and then he comes back and caches the other, covering it with sticks and leaves and dirt, concealing it from predators.

A while later, the young bear creeps back to the campsite, sees the big red bear, and retreats, but not too far. When the big red bear leaves the cache in search of water in the creek below the campsite, the young bear hurries forward, gorging himself until he hears the big red bear returning.

Later that afternoon, quiet returns to the Grizzly Maze. The big red bear curls up atop its cache, and the young bear rests in a thicket a short distance away.

Introduction:
Killing Bears with Kindness

ON THE AFTERNOON OF SUNDAY, October 5, 2003, in Alaska's Katmai National Park, one or more brown bears killed and ate Timothy Treadwell, 46, and his girlfriend, Amie Huguenard, 37. Investigating authorities subsequently killed two bears that threatened them at Treadwell's campsite. It was later determined that one of the bears had human flesh and clothing in its stomach.

Thirteen years earlier, Treadwell, a bartender from Malibu, California, with a self-described drug and alcohol problem, had fled his troubles for the isolated coast of Southeast Alaska, apparently on a spiritual journey to find himself. His first trip to Alaska changed him—he said he found salvation in a near-death experience with a half-ton brown grizzly bear—and thereafter he dedicated his life to grizzly bears. He was passionate about saying he was defending them from poachers. Treadwell traveled to Alaska every summer for more than a dozen years, living in remote campsites among brown bears. He captured their activities in photos and videos and took notes on what he witnessed. Occasionally, to the amusement of some park rangers and bear biologists who got within sight of him, Tim even mimicked the behaviors of grizzly bears. Standing upright with his legs bent slightly and his arms and hands curled up against his chest, he would plant his feet at a 90 degree angle to the observers, swivel his upper body to face them for several seconds, then lope away, stopping every 50 yards to rear up and study them before continuing on his way.

After more than a decade in the area, Tim had begun to scoff at the experts' depiction of the grizzly bear as a dangerous animal. He suggested instead that the grizzly was more of a misunderstood, affectionate beast than a killer. Timothy Treadwell's emergence as a self-styled bear expert coincided with a rising national fascination with the grizzly bear. Today hundreds of thousands of tourists vacation annually in

Alaska's national parks, many thousands of them participating in commercial bear-viewing excursions. The more adventuresome eco-tourists actually tread tentatively through grizzly country—fearful, yet hopeful of catching a glimpse of this great beast, even at their peril.

But Treadwell alienated the close-knit fraternity of bear experts by further suggesting that grizzly bears will eventually accept, even welcome, the close presence of non-threatening humans. And many bear experts were dismayed by his mercurial rise in popularity and alarmed at the message he was spreading. Treadwell appeared on such television programs as *Dateline NBC, The Late Show with David Letterman,* and the *Rosie O'Donnell* show. The Discovery Channel broadcast a film about him and showed him moving within arm's reach of half-ton grizzly bears, to the consternation of the experts.

Treadwell's supporters claim he possessed a special gift, while most professional bear biologists and even many Alaskans predicted it was only a matter of time before Timothy's end would come. His most fervent supporters feared poachers; his critics, a bear attack.

Depending on which camp has the floor, Treadwell has been either castigated for his irresponsible actions or praised for his passionate, reckless bravery to save an endangered animal; in the face of his death, the controversy rages on. Both supporters and critics openly predicted his demise, and when it came, it brought no closure to the debate.

Was Timothy Treadwell so wrong about grizzly bears that he had to die under the ripping claws and tearing jaws of one of the bears he loved so much? Did Amie Huguenard, who had voiced her fears to Tim about getting so close to the bears in the days before her death, have to die, either? Or the bears found feeding on their remains? If these deaths were not a foregone conclusion, where does the responsibility for them lie? That's a controversial question with complicated answers.

Explaining the human attraction to grizzly bears is like trying to grab a fistful of night breeze wafting through the pines. Is it as simple as our desire to behold the stateliness and resolute dignity of this great beast that is exponentially bigger, faster, stronger than we are? Or do we seek, by capturing it in our gaze, to divest the bear of its stateliness and shore up our own flagging morale?

Whatever it is, I've got it bad. I seek out grizzly country every chance I get. For me, just to be there is enough. On a recent trip to Kodiak Island, my friend Mark Matheny and I hiked for days over a hundred miles of brown grizzly bear country. We hiked along high ridges and sloshed through dense swamps, advanced along alder-choked salmon streams and through brooding rain forests of Sitka spruce and hemlock. We found fresh bear droppings and heard brush snapping. We found day beds of matted grass and studied rub trees worn slick, with long strands of coarse brown hair stuck to the bark 8 feet above the ground. We carried bear pepper spray, sometimes in extended hands, while we pushed through dense cover. In four days of hiking we never saw a bear. Was I disappointed? Heck no! We were in the king's palace. That reverence for bears, and a deep understanding of the attractions of the Alaskan wilderness, I took as my starting point in unraveling the story of Timothy Treadwell.

–Mike Lapinski, November 2004
Superior, Montana

CHAPTER 1

Breaking All the Rules in Bear Country

It was finally dark. . . . Suddenly, I felt the ground start to shake from the paws of a big bear. Then I heard the swish and crush of tall grass being trampled. A bear was bedding down for the evening. Without alarm I left the tent, shining my flashlight into the pitch-black evening. Gradually, I maneuvered the bright light in the direction of the visitor. . . . Mr. Chocolate, my beautiful friend, had stopped by to spend the night.

—Timothy Treadwell and Jewel Palovak,
*Among Grizzlies: Living with Wild Bears
in Alaska*

IN JULY OF 2000 GEORGE TULLOS, a 41-year-old Alaskan native, pitched his tent at the Run Amock Campground northeast of Ketchikan and crawled into his tent, feeling snug and safe after a long day of bear watching.

And why not? He was in a well-used camping area and was spending the night in a place where the big brown coastal grizzly bears were thought to be benign because they were so well fed. Thousands of spawned-out salmon clogged the nearby river and provided an abundance of food for the bears. The spot was considered so safe that the Forest Service maintained a bear-viewing platform 3 miles away along the river, where people could watch bears passing by as close as 20 yards away as the bloated bruins blissfully gorged on dead salmon.

Tullos was stirred awake during the night by the shaking of the ground and the crush of grass outside his tent. He probably poked his head outside his tent with flashlight in hand. The next morning, a passerby found the Tullos campsite torn apart, and investigating rangers discovered the partially eaten body of George Tullos. A short time later, they encountered a brown bear and killed it. A necropsy found human flesh in its belly, along with berries and grass.

In another part of Alaska, at another time, Timothy Treadwell would emerge from his tent stretching and yawning, and then he set out to find his "good friend" Mr. Chocolate among the dozens of brown bears roaming within a mile of his campsite. Ironically, George Tullos, who always kept a clean camp and made it a practice to observe bears at a distance, fell victim to claw and fang, while for many years Timothy Treadwell lived, despite the fact that he'd repeatedly violated most of the rules for proper behavior in bear country.*

Timothy ignored basic bear-aware rules (such as never approach a bear and avoid areas frequented by bears) at first out of ignorance; later he acted out of a growing conviction that the bears accepted and trusted him. Beginning with his very first foray into bear country, Timothy exhibited a disturbing lack of judgment, largely attributable to his admitted naiveté as an outdoorsman, and for years he not only got away with it, he was celebrated for it. But all did not start smoothly for Timothy Treadwell when he first arrived in Alaska.

Shortly after lunch on a drizzly afternoon in Katmai National Park in 1989, Timothy hiked along a major bear trail and began to

---

*It's not as if no guidelines exist concerning proper human behavior in bear habitats. Since 1988 the Center for Wildlife Information has distributed millions of brochures and quick-reference reader cards to help people traveling through bear country enjoy their stay while keeping themselves and the bears safe and stress-free.
- Never approach a bear
- Always view bears from a safe distance
- Eliminate food and its odor from camp
- Avoid areas frequented by bears
- Never hike in the dark in bear country
- Carry bear-deterrent pepper spray

find huge piles of bear droppings, black and squishy from fish oil. He waited for hours at a place where the trail followed a river, but no bears appeared. In the book he coauthored with Jewel Palovak, *Among Grizzlies*, Timothy penned his thoughts: "Hours passed, and not a single bear visited. Showers came and went. When it wasn't raining, mosquitoes dined on any exposed area of my body. . . . The rain forced other bugs into hiding, but caused its own obvious misery. My flimsy rain gear left me soaking wet. . . . Tears of frustration welled up in my eyes. All I wanted was the company of bears."

As the long Alaska light faded at about 11 P.M., Timothy started back to camp along the gloomy forest trail he'd traveled hours earlier, the path now dark and slick in the pouring rain. Suddenly, branches snapped and cracked just ahead. Timothy Treadwell was about to get his wish.

Out of the dim pathway ambled two massive bears directly in Treadwell's way. Singing softly but shaking with adrenaline and fear, Timothy backed away slowly, feeling successful and, in fact, elated when each bear veered away from him into the brush. Then the real test of Timothy's nerve came lumbering down the trail. A third bear entered the pathway. This bear was one of those thousand-pound brutes that, even on all fours, can stand as high as a man's head. As the bear swaggered toward him, Timothy began backing up and singing songs. The bear moved faster forward than Timothy could travel backward, though, and Timothy stumbled as the bear closed the gap. The muddy earth sent his feet out from under him, and he landed face first in the black mire. Timothy curled into a fetal position, trembling while the big bear stood hovering above him, so close that Tim could smell the stench of fish on the bear's breath.

Despite being petrified, Timothy peeked a glance up at the bear and saw long scars running across the old bear's face and "pearl-dagger" claws that could tear him apart. But instead of attacking, the big bear carefully stepped over the quaking body of Timothy Treadwell, actually brushing Tim's shoulder with its belly as it passed.

Long after the bear was out of sight, Timothy stayed trembling on the trail, frightened but exuberant that a bear had come so close without hurting him. As night enveloped the trail, Timothy Treadwell retraced his steps through the woods, chanting "thank you bears, thank you" to the beasts he thought he understood.

On his very first outing, Timothy Treadwell had violated two cardinal rules: Never hike in the dark, and always view bears from a safe distance. Bear experts often don't even bother to warn hikers about traveling through bear country in the dark because the danger is so obvious.* Even in the daytime a brown bear at rest in dense brush can be nearly invisible.

In retrospect it might have been a lifesaving, though painful, experience at that embryonic stage of his bear vision quest if that half-ton grizzly had swatted Timothy Treadwell with a sledgehammer-like blow and busted a half dozen of his ribs, or shaken him like a rat while crushing the bones in his shoulder.

But Timothy got lucky. The bear passed without incident, no doubt bolstering his budding notion that if we humans love bears, they'll love us back. He was hooked on the experience of getting close to grizzlies and would continue to do so for more than ten years, camping among them each summer at Katmai National Park. Timothy moved toward bears over and over again without being attacked, though he had many close calls. In one day a single bear charged him three different times, and those episodes subsequently brought Timothy fame among bear lovers while incurring the dismay of bear experts.

Located 30 miles west of Kodiak Island via the Shelikof Strait, Katmai National Park was originally designated a national monument

---

*Ninety percent of all attacks by grizzly bears occur when a human suddenly encounters the bear within 40 yards, which triggers an aggressive/defensive reaction in the bear. This terminology describes a behavior that occurs when a startled bear is actually fearful of being harmed and rushes forward to neutralize the danger before running off. Lacking the night vision of an animal, humans in the dark run the risk of overlooking a nearby bear, and are likely to walk right into trouble.

in 1918 in order to preserve the famed Valley of Ten Thousand Smokes, a spectacular forty-square-mile pyroclastic ash flow deposited by the Novarupta volcano. (Currently, fourteen of the volcanoes in Katmai are considered active, though none are currently erupting.) It's no surprise that Timothy Treadwell eventually chose Katmai National Park for the staging ground of his star-crossed odyssey. It had everything he needed: fantastic scenery, wilderness, isolation, lots of big brown bears—and a perplexingly cordial staff. Katmai, as it turned out, was the perfect location for achieving the closeness he craved with bears.

When it first became a national monument, Katmai had received some attention from geologists and volcano lovers, but in its early years the number of visitors didn't come close to matching the enviable attendance record of Denali, its sister park to the northeast. Even by 1980, when the nearly five million-acre area was finally designated a national park, Katmai took a backseat, in terms of visitors, to Denali. There, tens of thousands of animal lovers vied for the privilege of viewing its wildlife. Visitors to Katmai were relatively few, although the numbers grew from 2,200 visitors to the NPS Brooks Camp Visitor Center in 1980 to 5,800 visitors in 1990, the year Timothy Treadwell first arrived in the park. The difference in popularity wasn't that Katmai didn't have bears. More than 2,000 of the giant brown bears roamed Katmai's shores and inland forests, sustained by a series of salmon spawning runs that saw millions of the dying fish struggling up its numerous freshwater streams that flow into the ocean. The big problem at Katmai was access. It was truly a wilderness park, with no roads slicing through the heart of it like at Denali. At Katmai visitors either flew or boated to get anywhere in the park, and then they were stuck there until they flew or boated out.

Katmai was discovered by the tourism trade after the *Exxon Valdez* ran aground in Prince William Sound. That catastrophic oil spill in March 1989 threatened to destroy hundreds of miles of pristine Alaskan shoreline. Desperate federal officials sent urgent pleas for all charter craft to aid in corralling the spreading black oil slick. Lured by the promise of big bucks, fishing and sightseeing boats steamed down the Shelikof Strait to help with the oil cleanup.

It was during these trips back and forth along the Katmai Coast that charter boat captains noticed the large numbers of brown bears roaming in plain view along the shore. After the oil spill was contained, many of the more enterprising boat captains began offering bear-viewing excursions. Land excursions led by experienced bear guides were added to the eco-tourism options, and tourism exploded to more than 30,000 each year by 2004, with seventy commercial operators of bear-viewing excursions working within park boundaries.

Initially, bear-viewing rules and regulations were few at Katmai because almost all of the bear viewing occurred from boat or plane. Overnight stays were a rarity, and Katmai didn't even require a backcountry camping permit, except in certain areas. By contrast, Denali has always required anyone planning a camping trip to apply for a backcountry camping permit and attend a half-hour training session. In Denali visitors are not allowed to move closer than a quarter mile (1,400 feet) from any grizzly bear. In Katmai the rules allow visitors to approach up to 100 yards of female bears with cubs and 50 yards of all other bears.

Almost from the first day Timothy Treadwell set foot in Katmai National Park, he seemed to have had a deep, dedicated commitment to the park and its bears. However, his early visits were most notable not for his interactions with bears but for his struggles to survive the harsh living conditions along the Katmai Coast.

Mark Emery, a wildlife filmmaker and outdoor guide, remembers the day when he was on a charter flight across Katmai National Park, and he saw a solitary figure frantically waving his arms skyward.

The plane landed, and a desperate, frightened Timothy Treadwell rushed forward and asked to be taken away right then and there. "He said the bears had invaded his camp," Emery recalled. "They chewed up everything. I took a picture of Timothy holding a water can that was crushed by a bear and had big teeth holes in it. There was a fresh-water stream close by, but he just wanted away from those bears. I was with a film crew from *National Geographic*, and we had a schedule to keep, but we contacted a charter service and they came in and picked him up."

But Timothy soon grew bolder around the bears. Typical of his behavior in Katmai was a foray he took one morning in the Grizzly Sanctuary at Hallo Bay, during which he encountered scores of bears feeding on grass. In his book *Among Grizzlies*, Timothy described the event: "The sprawling green fields were littered with bears. One patch boasted between forty and fifty bears. . . . I slowly made my way onto the green, staying a comfortable hundred yards away for relatively safe viewing. Slinking about, I discovered a large crater surrounded by fresh piles of bear droppings. . . . I recognized the crater . . . as being a bear daybed. . . . I plopped down in the crater, and peeked out over the edge at the bears. I couldn't believe it! If anyone had ever told me that one day I'd be lying in a real grizzly bear bed with fifty of them surrounding me, I'd have thought they were crazy."

Timothy soaked up the experience, vowing in those moments to bring what he was learning back to the outside world. When he safely surrendered his spot in the bedding ground to "Mr. Chocolate," he was euphoric, believing that the bears trusted him enough to share their habitat with him so intimately.

But the bear experts were not pleased. When they saw or had word of his activities, some of these experts called Timothy's practice of moving close in to the bears crazy and stupid. Biologists such as Sterling Miller, then an Alaska Department of Fish and Game biologist, and Tom Smith, a research wildlife biologist for the U.S. Geological Survey Alaska Science Center, counseled Timothy about the messages he had begun to send to the public. Depending upon his mood, Timothy either agreed and said he would stop doing it or he blew them off with remarks like, "The bears know me and trust me." Even those few bear experts who felt affection for Timothy warned him about the effects and consequences of moving in close to bears. Bear folk hero and writer Doug Peacock warned Timothy that he was taking the bears too lightly and that he was maybe sending the wrong message to the public.

Tim's erratic behavior eventually brought him much attention. Wildlife photographer Alan Sanders, an experienced backpacker, often queried Timothy about his living conditions. "He never put a shine on his early days, at least to me," Sanders says. "A lot of times he was cold, hungry, bug bit, and scared to death. But year after year he kept coming back. Aboriginal natives in similar conditions built wood or sod shelters. Not Tim; he wanted to have a purely wilderness experience. Like he mentioned in his book, I think he wanted to be a bear."

Bear-viewing tour guides began approaching park rangers with tales of a weird guy acting like a bear and running away, or screaming curses at other bear viewers, or sneaking around and scaring bear-viewing parties.

Biologist Tom Smith reported that he often saw "Timmy the bear," as he called him. "He wouldn't come to me. He'd run away like a bear. He was a nut, but there's lots of them out there. I kind of liked the guy. I'd seek him out whenever I saw him, whether he wanted it or not.

"One time there were two of us [bear biologists] walking along the beach, and we found a dead brown bear cub. Its mouth was full of porcupine quills. Timothy's camp was only about a hundred yards away, so we walked over to it and I called his name. I knew he was in there, but he didn't respond. He was strange that way. I finally shook the tent pole and yelled, 'I know you're in there, Tim. Come on out. One of your bears is dead.' Well, he shot right out of the tent and I told him, with tongue in cheek, 'Tim, you're supposed to be protecting these bears, but you're not doing a very good job of it. I just found a dead cub a hundred yards away from your tent.' Tim got all serious and spread his arms and said, 'Hey, that's nature!' "

As Timothy Treadwell's name popped up more and more on park rangers' complaint sheets, they started keeping an eye on this strange bear-man. One behavior they noticed right off: Treadwell was getting way too close to the bears. Sometimes he was even camping right on top of bear feeding areas. Though he was never cited for it, rangers often warned him to stay back from the bears. They asked him to stop stressing the bears with his hovering presence. Depending upon the day and the particular ranger, Timothy might be friendly and accommodating or moody and belligerent.

When Deb Liggett took over as Katmai National Park superintendent in 1997, the park staff set up a meeting specifically to fill her in about Timothy Treadwell, who by then had created quite a rift between himself and the bear-viewing operators in Homer. Timothy had been threatened with bodily harm by an irate bear-viewing guide after he had chased away bears to "keep them safe" from the guide's half-dozen urban tourists.

Another commercial bear-viewing guide filed a harassment complaint with Katmai Park against Timothy after an altercation, during which the complainant alleged that Treadwell became belligerent and threatening. However, Timothy's take on the incident was decidedly different. In a letter to Superintendent Liggett dated August 25, 2000, he wrote," I was in a neutral area to record on video the activity. The guide was not pleased and approached me. I attempted to withdraw because past conversations with commercial operators have had poor results. Having heavy equipment, the guide almost caught up to me and we did have a simple and quiet conversation."

After rangers explained to Timothy that he had no legal right to harass or impede commercial bear-viewing guides, Timothy became more accommodating of the steady stream of bear viewers, and the tension eventually eased.

Unfortunately, the bear harassment problems with Timothy did not ease. Rangers were constantly shooing Timothy away from bears who wanted to be left alone, and who showed obvious signs of being stressed. When Treadwell's book, *Among Grizzlies*, was published in 1997, park personnel were startled by his multiple accounts of moving to within mere feet not only of submissive young females but also of female bears with cubs and even dominant adult males.

In the summer of 1998, park rangers began asserting their legal muscle. Rangers questioned Timothy four times at his camp about his food storage practices, and each time Timothy swore that he was complying with park requirements. Rangers inspected his camp while Treadwell was away and found an ice chest containing food in his tent, a violation of park rules. When the rangers looked under a tarp in front of his tent, they found a box of canned fruit and a case of Coca-Cola. They then followed a footpath away from his tent and in a grove of trees discovered a portable generator, which was prohibited in a wilderness area.

While accepting responsibility for leaving his food unsecured in his tent, Timothy was less than contrite when he wrote a long, rambling letter of protest to the superintendent dated June 23, 1998. An excerpt pertaining to the citation states, "I went for a brief washing in a freshwater creek. I left the cooler in the tent without duck [sic] taping it [park rules require food to be sealed in odor-proof, bear-proof containers]. I was wrong. I am sorry. What concerns me is this. Without ever asking, the rangers unzipped my secure tent and went through my belongings. I am outraged and hurt."

Deb Liggett decided that something had to be done about Timothy Treadwell, or she was going to have an injured bear whisperer and some dead bears on her hands. She phoned several of Timothy's acquaintances and asked the question, "What would get Timothy Treadwell's attention?"

They responded, "Threaten to kick him out of the park."

CHAPTER 2

Timothy Treadwell's Rise to Prominence

WHEN TIMOTHY TREADWELL arrived in Alaska in 1989 at the age of 33, his first stop was at Wrangell–St. Elias National Park, east of Anchorage. There he had his first bear encounter, but he was disappointed because the bear ran away from him. According to Timothy's own account, he was a burned-out drug addict who pulled himself out of the morass of drugs and ventured into the wilds of Alaska where he found a new life in the presence of the grizzly bear. But according to some who knew him, he wasn't an addict at all. He was just a trouble-making punk who got crossways with some drug dealers for some other reason and fled to Alaska to escape their wrath. At various times Tim claimed that he was an orphan, that he had been born in Australia, that he was estranged from his family, that he had been born in 1961. None of these assertions proved to be true. So who was Timothy Treadwell the man? And how did a self-described alcoholic, hyperactive street punk with no scientific training become a well-known bear celebrity in just a few short years?

After leaving Wrangell–St. Elias National Park, Timothy then booked a flight on a float plane that took him west to the remote wilderness of Alaska's Katmai National Park, and it was there that Timothy had his life-altering brown bear encounters. Timothy's first year in Alaska was relatively insignificant when compared to following years, though some may counter that a thousand-pound grizzly's belly scraping against your shoulder as it steps over you can hardly be called insignificant. In any case Timothy returned to California in the fall of 1989 and worked diligently to save money for his next year's trip. His binge drinking continued, however, and he admitted that he was always on edge, ready to fight with anyone who looked at him the wrong way.

During those winter months he visited the library to learn more about grizzly bears. In a book about Katmai National Park, he learned of an area in the park that was supposed to harbor plenty of bears, and that's where he headed in early summer 1990. Timothy had an agenda from the day the float plane dropped him off at the secluded bay he later named the Grizzly Sanctuary, and he went about accomplishing it among the thirty or so bears who inhabited the area near Hallo Bay. Armed with a camera and a can of pepper spray, he set out to immerse himself in the grizzly world. As he sat on the bank of a roiling river, the thick brush behind him began to snap. Thirty feet away, a 300-pound golden-brown bear stepped into the open and began moving toward him. Most people would have backed away and given the bear some space. Not Timothy. According to his later writing in *Among Grizzlies*, he sat and watched the bear from a distance of less than 20 feet, crooning to it, "I love you."

His account continued, "As I poured out my heart, the bear relaxed, and seemed to be enjoying the moment. . . . Suddenly, a name for the bear came to me." He spoke to the bear again: "You're just a little Booble, aren't you? . . . I love you, Booble."

Timothy laid a human name on the very first bear he met at Katmai and immediately began his purposeful descent into anthropomorphism and the fulfilling of his agenda to reinvent the grizzly bear in a kinder, gentler form, claiming that he was conducting original, ground-breaking research. Tim misinterpreted the smallest action by a bear as a human-like act of either trust or affection. In one instance, after Tim had tearfully confessed his addiction to alcohol and his determination to rid himself of it to the nearby feeding bear he'd named Booble, Tim wrote in *Among Grizzlies*, "Booble watched me calmly, then did something extraordinary. With a playful swat, she flipped a clamshell over to me. Elated by the action, I picked up the shells and stuffed these treasures into my pocket."

Gary Porter, an Alaskan bush pilot who knew Tim and occasionally flew him in and out of Katmai, was quoted in an *Alaska* magazine article as saying: "I think Timmy made a fundamental anthropomorphic error. Naming them and hanging around with them as long as he did, he probably forgot that they were bears. And maybe they forgot, some of the time, he was human."

During Timothy's season-long visits to the Grizzly Sanctuary, he photographed bears, named them, and, as he claimed in *Among Grizzlies*, chased away poachers. He roamed the secluded bay relentlessly, not content to just observe the bears, but obsessed with getting close to them. Rarely did he sit back and merely watch. He nearly always chose instead to initiate some kind of contact with them. During those early years Timothy contacted a few other "bear people" who leaned toward unconventional behavior among bears. He often spoke with writer and photographer Charlie Russell, also a self-styled naturalist, who was famous for living among the grizzlies in Kamchatka, Russia. Tim also spoke with writer and documentary filmmaker Doug Peacock, who spent thirteen years camping among grizzlies in Montana and Wyoming before he wrote, in 1990, *Grizzly Years*. An outspoken advocate of wildlands preservation, Peacock also experienced a series of near-suicidal encounters with charging bears. Though the three men had much in common in terms of their close contact with brown bears in the wild, Russell and Peacock disagreed with Timothy on his treatment of bears as friends and family. Instead, they opted for a more realistic approach to safety. They used electric fences around their campsites and carried bear spray on their hips. But Timothy said he stopped carrying bear spray because he didn't want to hurt the bears, and he swore he'd never use an electric fence because he didn't want to hurt the bears' and the foxes' noses in any way.

The brown bears on Katmai are accustomed to human visitors; more than 55,000 tourists currently visit the park each season from May through October. But they're still wild bears, and more than once, Timothy learned that his intrusions into a bear's life were not appreciated. One day he encountered a 650-pound bear that appeared docile at first, but then the bear turned back to vanquish the human who was pressuring him. The bear's head was down and its ears were laid back as he moved directly at Timothy. But before the bear charged, Timothy turned on his bear act. He began to snarl and hiss, charging and kicking up mud. As the strange human bear came closer, the real bear lost its nerve and backed away submissively. And so began a very troubling tendency in Timothy Treadwell to sometimes charge at subadult bears that he thought were acting aggressively toward him. These were all close-range encounters and could easily have been avoided if the bears had not been stressed by Timothy's presence.

But Timothy's seeming ability to relate to these bears in human terms was exactly what propelled him into the limelight. When he returned to California, he worked as a bartender in Malibu and began showing his photos, which were sensational due to his close proximity to the bears. The movie stars, publicity agents, and film producers who stopped at the bar were captivated by his photos and bear tales. The attention was intoxicating to Timothy; combined with the thrill he received from his proximity to the bears, it fuelled his obsession further. Timothy returned to Alaska in 1991 and 1992, these times equipped with a video camera. When he returned home he had both photos and video to show the large enclave of celebrity animal-rights supporters in the Hollywood and Malibu areas. Timothy began to be invited to parties where he gave talks about the bears, and his own celebrity began to grow.

Now instead of holding a drink in his hand, he grasped his book of bear pictures to show to anyone who met his eyes. He was just as outgoing as ever, but now he was preaching the love of bears instead of just babbling as a drunk. His new passion drew the attention of

Jewel Palovak, a graduate of the University of Southern California and an ardent animal-rights activist. They'd known each other for several years, and their casual relationship grew into a deep friendship. Jewel liked what Timothy was saying about the grizzly bears he loved, and she especially liked what he had to say about stopping poachers and hunters from killing all the bears.

Even at this early stage of his newly envisioned career as an animal-rights activist, Timothy harbored visions of fame. He contacted Malibu film producer Peter Dixon. From his home in New Zealand, when asked about Treadwell, he recalled, "Timothy had just finished his first or second summer with the bears and realized he needed exposure if he was to continue his odyssey. . . . Of course, Timothy envisioned the film to be about him and his bears. That began a minor conflict of give-and-take, but he was mature enough to realize that he was not yet a media star." The result was a documentary titled *In the Land of the Grizzlies*. Tim's effusive, high-energy personality, combined with his blond surfer-dude good looks and athletic build, made him a natural in front of a camera, and audiences wanted more.

Nature program producers know what it takes to film a successful program—a charismatic lead character, an interesting fast-paced story, beautiful scenery, and wildlife. With Timothy Treadwell they got it all: a human-interest story about an alleged drug addict rededicating his life to saving bears from poachers, beautiful Alaskan scenery, and powerful brown bears. With Timothy it was obvious from the start that he did not fear the big brown bears he continually moved in on. The viewer saw only that this was not faked. These were real bears, and every moment that Timothy spent close to one could be his last. Timothy Treadwell was a nature producer's dream.

After the Audubon Society produced a video featuring Tim, he began to associate more with the very determined Jewel Palovak. They coordinated a plan to force the State of California to ban the steel leg-hold trap. They joined in anti-hunting rallies. Timothy's star would probably not have risen so fast without Jewel's organizing force.

While Timothy went through mood swings and affairs and estrangements, Jewel began passing his name and exploits among the upper reaches of society that she often moved in in her role as someone in the vanguard of animal rights. In 1994 she managed to get a short profile of Timothy published in *People* magazine, followed by a book contract from HarperCollins. But Timothy was woefully ill-suited for the enormous responsibility and discipline needed to write a book. Jewel took over and became his coauthor. *Among Grizzlies: Living with Wild Bears in Alaska* hit the stores in 1997.

Sales were moderate, but all that changed when Timothy appeared on the *Tom Snyder Show* in 1998. With blond hair drooping over his eyes and his cap on backwards, Timothy rolled his eyes and gestured wildly while he explained his bear research. "I'm like this animal that's always safe, always kind."

The program then switched to footage of a fat butterball of a bear in a stream eating a salmon. Nearby, Timothy sang, "Hi Cracker. I love you, Cracker."

Back to the studio, Timothy brought up the issue that would become his mantra. "My biggest job is to watch over them [bears] about poachers."

"Really?" Snyder erupted in surprise.

"Yeah. People will try to kill them for a trophy, for a thrill kill, which really bums me out, or for their body parts, like their gall bladders that bring thousands of dollars in the Asian markets."

Snyder changed the subject and asked, "Now, when these bears get used to you and your presence there, do they ever go about their life like you weren't there?"

"That's exactly what it is!" Timothy jumped in with an eager nod of his head. "And it's . . ." He stumbled over the right words to explain his actions. "It's not really habituation like other people do. I am one of them. They know I'm safe and I'm kind."

Snyder then rolled the next footage, which showed Timothy sitting on a rock in a stream barely 10 feet from a bear he had named

Tabitha. On the film he turns his back on the bear and begins reading aloud from his book to the seemingly disinterested animal.

Back at the studio, Snyder asked Timothy if the bears ever mate in front of him, and Timothy explained that he once watched two bears mate over the course of twenty-one days. Snyder jumped in and asked with a smirk, "Have you ever mated among them?"

Caught off guard, Timothy hesitated, then jumped in and enthusiastically replied with a lurid roll of his eyes, "Well, there was a time two years ago when I had a girlfriend up there and we, well, uh, her family might be watching so I shouldn't say more."

Then Timothy abruptly returned to his agenda. "Did you know in Yellowstone they're trying to delist the grizzly? And as soon as they delist it, they're going to begin a sport hunt."

"Really!" Snyder asked, aghast.

"Yes," Timothy replied with a somber nod. "As a thrill kill, for no other reason than a decoration, and I hope America stands up to stop it and save the bear."

"Me, too!" Snyder blurted. "Me, too!"

The Tom Snyder interview was a rousing success, propelling Timothy into the limelight, and book sales surged.

That segment was followed that same year with a *Dateline NBC* segment, "Gentle Tim." Stone Phillips introduced him during a *Dateline NBC* segment. "Usually when we hear about the mightly grizzly, it's about a harrowing grizzly bear attack. But is that typical? A man you're about to meet says no. . . . He's part Dr. Doolittle, part Grizzly Adams, and to prove it he also lives with them and talks to them and crawls around on all fours like them." And with his patented Stone Phillips nod, he announced softly, "Meet Gentle Tim."

When reporter Keith Morrison interviewed Timothy during the program, he couldn't hide his chagrin after he viewed Timothy within mere feet of a half-ton bear. "This is crazy! This is nuts!" he blurted out. "These bears can break you in half like a match stick."

Timothy smiled knowingly and replied in a soft voice, "I think they've been misunderstood." And then with conviction he added, "This is a lifelong mission. I won't rest until all the bears are safe from man."

His mission was further explored in the 1999 Discovery Channel program *Grizzly Diaries*, for the most part a raw, primal look at the real life of grizzly bears. And to his credit, Timothy did very little crooning to the bears in the film, for once choosing to move aside and allow the bears to reveal the continuing life cycles played out each fall in grizzly country. But most knowledgeable bear people were still uncomfortable with his closeness to the bears. Didn't he realize that at any moment one of those bears that had been fighting and biting another bear could just as easily run over and end his life with one mighty swipe?

Between *Dateline NBC* and *Grizzly Diaries*, it appeared that Tim finally had the legitimacy he so desperately sought. Jewel and Tim formed a grassroots organization they called Grizzly People. Essentially a fund-raising apparatus for Treadwell's trips, Grizzly People was headquartered in Palovak's kitchen. Jewel created a Web site that offered Timothy's photographs for sale to finance his "expeditions," as he now called them. In the meantime Jewel was gathering generous donations from movie stars with an environmental bent. Actor Leonardo DiCaprio, who has his own nature Web site, donated almost $25,000 to Grizzly People. Other celebrities, including actor Pierce Brosnan, model Gisele Bundchen, and screenwriter Robert Towne, also donated funds, as did several large corporate sponsors such as Minolta, Konica, and Patagonia.

Colorado resident Roland Dixon, a bear lover who puts his money where his mouth is, learned about Timothy Treadwell from Charlie Russell, author of the 1999 book *Spirit Bear: Encounters with the White Bear of the Western Rainforest*, which explores the habitat and lives of British Columbia's rare white Kermode bears. Charlie Russell had told Roland that Timothy was working in Katmai to save bears from poachers and that Treadwell wanted to educate the public about the grizzly being shy and reclusive, rather than dangerous and a killer. Roland liked what he heard and phoned Timothy. Impressed with Timothy's excitement and love for the great bear, and his willingness to talk about "his" bears for hours, Roland decided to support both Timothy's expeditions and Grizzly People financially.

With Timothy's newfound celebrity status and financial stability, he became involved in other animal-rights causes. He went to Newfoundland to protect baby harp seals and showed every indication that he might switch at least some of his efforts to this endeavor.

Thanks to Jewel's persistence and connections, Timothy received a huge break in 2001 when David Letterman, always on the lookout for offbeat stories and characters, came calling. This was Timothy's big chance and he aced it, trading quips and barbs and more bear-poaching references with the king of late-night television. After running a film segment that showed Timothy moving dangerously close to brown bears, Letterman held up a photograph of a huge brown bear and asked, "One day are we going to read that one of these bears killed and ate you?" Timothy shrugged and replied, "This is dangerous work." Letterman liked Timothy's zany, devil-may-care attitude toward the danger of moving close to the big brown bears so much that he had him return a second time. Tim had become the poster boy for a new breed of entertainer-educators—the wildlife celebrity.

While Tim was doing all the talking, many bear experts were seething. At one point in his segment on *Late Night with David Letterman*, Timothy blurted out, "They're party animals. They just like to lay around and have a good time." It was a remark that would come back to haunt him, for it solidified the opposition of many wildlife biologists against Timothy for making such a cavalier statement about a potentially dangerous animal.

Bear biologist Tom Smith assessed Tim's relationship with the bears thusly, "All he was doing was harassing them. He said he was studying them, but he was just stressing them out by moving in so close to them."

But for many bear experts Timothy's personal encounters with the bears were not as disturbing as the misinformation he was spreading to the public. Timothy claimed he was protecting the bears from poachers, but there had never been a confirmed case of poaching in Katmai National Park, where dedicated park rangers patrolled constantly and where firearms were not even allowed.

The brazen statement that Timothy made on *Tom Snyder Show* about attempts to delist the grizzly in Yellowstone National Park, where grizzlies are protected by federal law, was not true and should have been corrected by Snyder—either at the moment or during the next show as a disclaimer. Instead it was ignored, leaving millions of viewers believing that hunters would soon descend upon a treasured national park with guns blazing.

As director of the Center for Wildlife Information (CWI), it's Chuck Bartlebaugh's job to be on the lookout for inaccurate or misleading information about wildlife, especially bears. CWI was already aware of Treadwell's exploits through his book, *Among Grizzlies*, and a CWI representative attended a bear symposium where Tim spoke and showed slides. Concerned that Tim was giving an inappropriate message about moving close to and communicating with bears, Chuck had previously contacted Timothy and explained to him that what he was preaching was completely against everything state and federal land management agencies were teaching about bears. "Tim was defensive and testy when I first confronted him about his actions being bad for people and bad for bears," Chuck recalled. "But then he backed off and became apologetic, saying that he didn't mean to misinform people, that he just wanted to show that the bears weren't dangerous."

CWI monitored Treadwell's speaking engagements, and when they learned that he would appear on the *Tom Snyder Show*, Chuck phoned the producer three weeks before the interview. "I told the producer that what Timothy was doing was against what every wildlife agency taught, and that Katmai National Park was against what he was doing up there. The producer promised to give me a chance to counter on the phone what Timothy said on the show. I got put on hold during the show and waited and waited, but they never did connect me."

However, Chuck's phone call to Timothy opened a line of communication between the two men that appeared to bear fruit. Chuck succeeded in getting Tim to agree to stop showing some of his closest-in footage. "I had to fight tooth and nail to stop Tim's *Tom Snyder Show* segment from re-running," recalled Chuck. "But I finally did stop it from being re-aired."

Because of Timothy's rapidly growing recognition, the National Park Service at one point considered using Timothy's rising stardom to its advantage by having him act as a spokesperson. But the problem of his unacceptable behavior of moving in close to bears remained an issue. Katmai superintendent Deb Liggett phoned Chuck Bartlebaugh and asked if he could speak with Tim and somehow dissuade him from acting irresponsibly around bears. His repeated questionable behavior around bears in Katmai was being reported by rangers, tourists, and bear-viewing guides. One photographer, in a June 1998 letter to park officials, complained that he watched Timothy straddle a sleeping bear and photograph it. Eventually, the National Park Service abandoned the idea of using Treadwell as a spokesperson.

In the fickle world of California celebrities, Timothy Treadwell seemed to be doing quite well. Accolades began to arrive. Noted paleontologist Louise Leakey wrote a letter to President George H. W. Bush asking him to support Timothy's passionate efforts to help save the great bears of the world. Indeed, the world of eco-warriors, monied supporters of wildlife causes, and enthusiastic groupies embraced him. Timothy continued going to Alaska and moving close to bears, much to the consternation of Katmai Park officials and professional bear experts. To them and even to the ordinary citizens of Alaska and other places where Treadwell's story had been aired, he was a nut—a showoff and a crazy man with a death wish.

But Tim's harshest critics were the very people he desired to impress the most: the bear experts. Bear biologists soundly condemned Timothy's flamboyant style around bears and his seemingly perverse obsession with getting close to the bears. In a 1999 bear symposium in Bozeman, Montana, Timothy nervously took the stage in front of hundreds of knowledgeable bear people and attempted to charm them, but his efforts fell flat. Respected bear expert Charles Jonkel stood and announced, "Timothy, I have some real problems with your behavior around bears."

Timothy almost fell over himself rushing into the audience to meet Jonkel. He apologized for his actions and explained that they were used merely to get people's attention to love the bears, and he stammered that he no longer moved close to bears, that he'd quit naming them, and that he was done with all the anthropomorphism and the hype and the glitz, and he just wanted to be friends and work to save the bears, and . . . It was the first time a professional bear biologist had taken a stand against Timothy Treadwell to his face, and Treadwell's response exposed a fragility beneath the dashing young man—he was able to blithely confront thousand-pound bears but wilted under criticism from humans.

Timothy's financial benefactor, Roland Dixon, invited him to Colorado to spread his message about bears to schoolchildren, and his schedule of school visits worked very well for a while. "Timmy was unbelievable," Dixon told me. "He was a human dynamo—go, go, go! But then he'd fall into that depression." That wasn't all that bothered Dixon about Timothy. He often behaved immaturely, blurting out statements that were contradictory, sometime false, and often times inflammatory. Dixon realized that Timothy needed to be brought under control. He needed legitimacy, validity, and consistency within the world of bear experts and bear habitat preservation activists.

Roland Dixon wasn't the only person trying to get Timothy under control. Katmai superintendent Deb Liggett was becoming increasingly concerned with the message Timothy was spreading to the public about moving in close to bears. She'd been in contact with The Center for Wildlife Information's Chuck Bartlebaugh about the matter and knew that the center possessed excellent bear safety literature, which it routinely customized for numerous state and federal land management and wildlife agencies. The center's message of bear safety was exactly what Deb Liggett wanted Timothy to be spreading.

In March 2000 Chuck Bartlebaugh answered the phone in his office and was surprised to hear Timothy Treadwell's voice. Chuck told me during our interview, "Tim explained that Deb Liggett had urged him to call me and get some help in putting out a better bear safety message or she was going to kick him out of Katmai. Tim said I should call his main financial benefactor, Roland Dixon, and see if we could figure out some program.

"I phoned Roland and he told me that Tim needed to be portrayed as being more professional and scientific. With Dixon's financial help, I agreed to assist Tim in developing new material that would help his image as a responsible bear expert."

Thus began a plan to furnish legitimacy to Timothy Treadwell by allowing him to use all The Center for Wildlife Information's literature. "I was pretty excited at that point," Chuck said, "because I knew that Tim could carry the message of wise bear stewardship into the glitzy places I couldn't penetrate."

While Timothy was in Colorado speaking to grade school children and college students about bears in the summer of 2000, Chuck met with Tim twice and ironed out plans to reinvent him as a legitimate player in the world of bear experts. In turn, Timothy promised that he would stop sending mixed messages about bear safety and humans.

In May 2001 Chuck attended the International Bear Conference in Jackson Hole, Wyoming. There had been some talk among biologists to issue a letter of censure concerning Timothy, and Chuck went to the conference to explain that he was working with Timothy to help him clean up his act. Chuck returned home and wrote a cordial letter to Roland Dixon informing him that no censorship had been discussed and that he was ready to insert photos of Timothy Treadwell and some of his bear photos into the newly developed literature.

Chuck waited for Timothy's photos. A week passed, then two, then three. Timothy never sent the photos. The opportunity passed.

When I interviewed Chuck Bartlebaugh shortly after Timothy's death, his face was drawn and his voice somber. "I felt we were real close to reaching Timothy and helping him. I should have tried harder; maybe I didn't explain clearly enough how the program of legitimacy would have worked to his benefit. I really feel like I've failed because now Timothy's dead, an innocent young woman is dead, and two grizzly bears are dead."

CHAPTER 3

The Subject of Poaching

DURING HIS INITIAL INTERVIEW with Tom Snyder on the *Tom Snyder Show*, emerging wildlife celebrity Timothy Treadwell quickly established his purpose for being among the bears. "My biggest job, my biggest duty, is to watch over them about poachers. People will try to kill them, either for a trophy or as a thrill kill, or for their body parts, for their gall bladder, which has been used in traditional medicine for almost 2,000 years," he said on the show, which aired in 1998.

Snyder asked, "Have you ever stepped between a poacher and a bear?"

"Yes," Timothy responded. "There's this bear named Tabitha, and one time this boat pulled up, and there were these men who looked like poster men for the NRA. They had machine guns and shotgun-type rifles and they were going to take her out, but I walked out and . . . I would take a bullet for Tabitha."

Calling upon the images of the evil hunter stalking the unsuspecting bear was Timothy Treadwell's bread and butter on the talk show and party circuit. The subject of poaching and his courageous crusade to protect the bears from poachers, always an emotional issue, was consistently woven through Timothy's public speeches and his television programs. And it worked. Several of his high-profile supporters mentioned the excellent job Timothy was doing in Katmai to suppress the poaching, citing as evidence the fact that there had not been a single poaching incident in the park in the thirteen years he'd been relentlessly patrolling its shores.

A true statement, agrees current Katmai superintendent Joe Fowler, but misleading, since poaching has been nonexistent throughout the park in the past twenty-five years. "But let's give Timothy credit on this one," Joe told me. "Timothy's presence certainly discouraged illegal activity. But not any more than any of the other 30,000 visitors who come here to view the bears.

"There's one thing I'd like to clear up about Timothy Treadwell. His book made it sound like he was camped out in some remote corner of the park where no one had ever visited, and where poachers roamed freely. He actually hung out in a very small area of the park, at a place that he code-named the Grizzly Sanctuary to discourage poachers from finding his bear Mecca at the big sedge grass field he called the Big Green. But everybody knows where the Big Green is. It's in Hallo Bay, a favorite place for bear viewers. I've seen a dozen or more bear-viewing boats docked there. A poacher would be nuts to try anything in that place. Those commercial bear-viewing guides make their living showing bears to people. They'd be all over anyone who tried to poach one."

Sterling Miller is a senior wildlife biologist for the National Wildlife Federation and former Alaska Fish and Game biologist who, along with fellow researcher Roy Smith, had been studying the brown bear populations for years before Timothy ever set foot in Katmai. He calls Treadwell's claims of poaching nonsense. "I was all over that country right after the *Exxon Valdez* oil spill in Prince William Sound. Our job was to study what effects the oil spill might have along the Katmai Coast. I was in and out of all that country. I beat a heck of a lot more brush than Timothy ever did. And I never saw one piece of evidence to support his claim—even back then."

In the 1960s and 1970s, poaching was not uncommon along the Alaskan Peninsula, of which Katmai National Park, despite its nearly five million acres, is but a very small part. Wealthy big-game trophy hunters from all over the world coveted the mighty brown bear. Unfortunately, the most desirable half-ton bears were not easy to come by in those areas open to legal bear hunting, so a few unscrupulous poachers sneaked into areas closed to bear hunting, including Katmai.

A favorite poaching story comes from a wealthy German man who hired a guide in 1974 to find him one of those fabled "big brownies." The guide took the hunter to a secluded bay in the dark and camouflaged the boat in the brush, explaining that the bears were so wary that even the sight of the boat was enough to send them into hiding. An hour later, the guide pointed out a huge brown bear moving along a brush-choked stream. The hunter dropped the big bear with a well-placed heart shot.

The guide barely allowed the successful hunter time to take a few pictures before he started peeling the hide from the bear. A storm was coming, he explained, and they had to work fast. When the sound of an airplane was heard, the guide frantically covered the bear with brush and started pushing the hunter into the dense alders.

"Why are you trying to hide?" the hunter asked.

"If we get caught here, we're in big trouble," the distraught guide blurted. "We're in Katmai National Park."

Former Katmai National Park superintendent Deb Liggett told me, "Katmai was just an isolated place back then, but after the *Exxon Valdez* disaster, a lot of contractors from Homer up north of the park were hired to clean up the mess, and it was while they were traveling along the Katmai Coast that they started seeing all the bears. It didn't take long before the place became a major bear-viewing destination. I think the last confirmed poaching incident was back in the 1970s. When I was superintendent there were no poaching incidents, nor was there any evidence of poaching. Timothy just had this agenda, and poaching seemed to fit into it."

Biologist Tom Smith, who roamed over much of Katmai before and during Timothy Treadwell's tenure there, also scoffs at Treadwell's poaching claims. "The place is flooded with bear-viewing and fishing boats, and there's constant air traffic above. How could anyone poach one without being seen? These are big animals. You don't just shoot one, throw it into the boat, and take off. I think the entire poaching claim was made up by Timothy Treadwell to further his cause of being the bears' protector."

In all fairness it should be noted that an occasional illegal killing does occur in grizzly country. When biologists were attempting to reintroduce a few grizzlies into northwest Montana's wild Yaak River country, their hard work was often thwarted. More than one of their radio-collared bears was found dead from a bullet wound. Neither the hide nor gall bladder was taken from these bears. They were killed by narrow-minded people opposed to the grizzly reintroduction plan. (The good news is that today the Yaak has a small but healthy grizzly population—the result of this project and also natural bear migration from Canada.)

One fact that Alaska wildlife managers like to stress is that the grizzly is not in danger of disappearing, nor is it being overhunted, legally or otherwise. Bruce Bartley, who monitors brown bear hunting harvests for the State of Alaska, informed me that while the state does allow brown bear hunting on the Alaskan Peninsula outside of the national park, it is tightly regulated. Of the approximately 40,000 grizzly bears living in the state, only about 1,400 are harvested annually. Of that total, the brown bear (coastal grizzly) take is about 400 bears each year.

"The grizzly population is very healthy," Bruce says. "We keep a pretty close eye on their numbers. Right now, we have almost too many bears. When the bears overpopulate an area, ungulates such as moose and caribou suffer. In some places where there are too many bears, it's hard for a calf moose to survive. The bears hunt and kill them in the spring. They don't just eat grass and fish, you know. If there's a moose or caribou or Sitka blacktail [a smallish deer native to Southeast Alaska] that they can take, they'll make a meal of it."

On the subject of bear poaching, Bruce Bartley reports, "We just don't have much. We have overhead flights, and any campsite is checked out from above. We take the protection of the grizzly very seriously, and so do the bear-hunting outfitters. They make their living doing it legally, and they'll turn in anyone poaching in heartbeat.

"The State of Alaska does allow some subsistence hunting in national parks that were created after 1980. This is strictly regulated and allotted mostly to Native Americans, but there are very few Indian villages along the Alaska Peninsula who eat brown bear meat because it is so rank with the taste of fish oil. Inland grizzlies that don't have access to salmon spawning runs have excellent meat, and these animals are . . . consumed by hunters.

"As far as poaching in Katmai National Park is concerned, I just don't think it's very likely that any poaching exists. The access is too difficult. You either have to fly in or boat in, and then there are people all over the place. That's not the way poachers work. They operate in places where there is quick road access. That way they'll go in, do their dirty work, and load a poached animal into a pickup and be gone quickly."

Bruce concedes that bears in remote areas of Russia may be at risk from poachers in search of legendary traditional cures. He says, "Bear poaching for the gall bladder has been, and still is, a problem in some places. The poor economy in Russia and the remoteness of the area where brown bears roam often lure poachers." Still, he points out reasons that poaching in Katmai is both unlikely and uneconomical: "A large brown bear's gall bladder might bring a couple hundred dollars, but the cost to poach one in Katmai is prohibitive, to say nothing of the legal hazards. You're going to pay anywhere from 600 to 800 dollars for a bush plane flight into Katmai."

Though bear experts scoffed at Timothy Treadwell's bear-poaching claims, bear lovers in the lower states took his claims seriously. Los Angeles school teacher Valerie Roach, whose fourth-grade class was visited by Treadwell and heard his story about protecting bears from poachers, became a staunch supporter of Timothy and even sent a donation to his Grizzly People Web site. She has maintained her support for him even after much of his work was questioned after his death. "He wasn't just photographing bears up there," she wrote in a letter that was published in the *Los Angeles Times,* "he was also protecting the bears from poachers."

Some simple arithmetic helps to address the poaching issue: For thirteen years Timothy Treadwell spent four months each year patrolling the Katmai Coast. That's fifty-two months. During that time Timothy recorded hundreds of hours of videotape and took thousands of photos—yet he never snapped a single photograph of the poachers against whom he claimed to be constantly on guard. As chance would have it, each time he apparently encountered a poacher, he didn't have his camera along.

Timothy's exasperation increased with the skepticism and sarcasm from bear experts, and from state and federal officials. There *were* bear poachers on Katmai, he protested. He claimed in *Among Grizzlies* that he had interviewed an anonymous convicted poacher who told Treadwell that he had killed more than a thousand grizzlies. The poacher's favorite killing ground was, by his own account, Timothy's Grizzly Sanctuary at Hallo Bay. But doubters only grew more open in their derision.

If there were poachers operating in Katmai, they wondered aloud with increasing frequency, why hadn't Timothy furnished proof?

So Timothy Treadwell went out and returned with what he claimed was irrefutable proof—a photograph of a poacher sneaking up on a bear at the Grizzly Sanctuary. Treadwell's Web site, Grizzly People, published the photo of a shotgun-toting man, with a caption proclaiming the man a bear poacher. One of Treadwell's main supporters, outdoor clothing giant Patagonia, sponsored and distributed an anti-poaching brochure that featured a photo of the man sneaking up on a protected Katmai bear. Treadwell supporters sniffed that an apology was in order and that it was time for the rest of the bear world to finally validate Timothy's efforts to save the bears. Timothy Treadwell, it seemed, was on the cusp of becoming a legitimate force in the bear world.

That is, until bear-viewing guide Joe Allen found out that *he* was the purported poacher. In his work as a commercial guide in Katmai,

Joe had met Timothy and had always had a cordial relationship with him. It was understandable that Joe would choke on his coffee when he picked up one of the Patagonia brochures and saw his picture plastered across the cover with the caption that he was an evil poacher.

Joe Allen's boss, Tom Walters, took this surprise even worse. Walters was co-owner of Katmai Wilderness Lodge and had befriended Treadwell when no one else would, providing him with food, clothing, and supplies. "He even stayed at my house when he flew with me," Tom fumed. "It was just a real cheesy thing he did. Joe Allen wouldn't hurt a fly. He knew Joe was no poacher, and he knew darn well there weren't any poachers out there in Katmai where he was."

Walters's attorney contacted Patagonia, and the company hastily retrieved and destroyed as many of the pamphlets as it could, but by then many had been issued to the public. Patagonia also pulled its financial support from Treadwell, though they eventually resumed it.

Butch Tovsen, a nature photographer who had shown Timothy where to find the bears when he first arrived in Alaska, and then flew him around from time to time for a few years, said, "Timothy Treadwell knew darn good and well that Joe Allen wasn't a poacher. He did the whole thing to keep the hype up."

Despite overwhelming evidence to the contrary, Timothy continued to push the poaching hype. In a September 2, 2003, letter to his California friends Marc and Marnie Gaede, he wrote: "I'm going to make it, unless one of the killer bears gets me. There are plenty this year. Lots of beautiful sweet bears, but as my work success takes greater affect [sic], more tough dominant giant bears come back . . . to their rightful place—to rule—free of poachers."

What agenda could Timothy Treadwell possibly have had that he would allow these claims to threaten—in fact, almost totally collapse—his credibility, if not with the public, then most certainly with the professional bear biologists whose approval he so desperately sought?

Famous bear biologists make only rare public appearances, especially on television, and most prefer to keep their work out of the limelight, in part because of the potentially dangerous nature of the bears they study. They fear that untrained members of the public will mimic their actions and get themselves and the bears in trouble, so they don't make guest appearances on late-night talk shows and they don't share their research with large numbers of laypeople. When bear biologists complete their field work, they issue a final report filled with pages of charts and graphs and endless data to support the study. Because they lack drama and excitement, these documents rarely find their way into the average public library, and therefore the growing numbers of bear lovers in the United States are deprived of information that would add to their understanding of the great bear.

Hundreds of federal, state, and private grants have been issued to study the grizzly, and academic libraries contain a treasure trove of information for the committed bear enthusiast, offering scientific, but often tedious, details on everything from bear mating habits and denning sites to analyses of their scat. These no-nonsense bear biologists labor in obscurity to improve habitat, security, and scientific knowledge of the grizzly. And they've done a good job. Today, for instance, more than a thousand grizzlies are living in the lower forty-eight states, and bears are moving into areas where they've been absent for decades.

Scientists haven't done too badly by the bears in Katmai, either, despite the claims Timothy Treadwell made, more than once, about the poor protection of bears in Alaska. In the eyes of the public, Timothy had become the unofficial protector of the Katmai bears and a student of their so-called secret ways, even though several studies by professional biologists had already been done there. In fact, the big male grizzly that was killed at the Treadwell campsite had study number 141 tattooed inside his lip, put there fifteen years earlier by state biologist Sterling Miller in nearby Kukak Bay.

So why did Timothy Treadwell continue to push his agenda in spite of the mountains of evidence that he was neither conducting new research nor protecting bears from poaching?

The answer may lie in a conversation I had with Grizzly People coordinator and cofounder, Jewel Palovak. In researching this book I'd already had a wonderful interview with Timothy's mother, Carol Dexter. And his chief financial supporter, Roland Dixon, had graciously provided many insights into Timothy. Toward the end of my phone conversation with Roland, he urged me to also speak with Jewel, just as Carol Dexter had. Roland provided Jewel's phone number and told me that he'd call ahead to pave the way for me. I was greatly appreciative of Roland's help, and I was personally excited to finally make contact with Jewel over the phone. She'd been such a huge part of the Timothy Treadwell story.

I phoned Jewel the next day, got the Grizzly People message machine, and left my name and phone number.

The next afternoon my phone rang, and a woman on the other end of the line said, "Hello, this is Jewel Palovak."

"Well, hello, Jewel," I said. "I'm so pleased to finally meet you. I was . . ."

"Listen," she cut me off. "I really don't think I want to be talking to you."

It would be an understatement to say that I was stunned. "Uh, why, Jewel?" I asked.

"Well, I checked you out on the Internet and I found out that you're a hunter and you trap, and that you hunt bears and kill bears, and you've written all these books about hunting. How could you have the nerve to call me up and ask for an interview?"

"Jewel," I stammered, "I don't see what . . ."

"Why didn't you have the decency to admit to Roland and Carol Dexter who you were? That you were a hunter. That you trapped, that you killed bears."

"Well, uh, I didn't think it mat . . ."

"Well let me tell you something. If I could somehow put an end to animal hunting, I'd die a happy person."

My shock was finally wearing off, and I was slowly beginning to understand where Jewel Palovak was coming from.

"Okay, Jewel, you've had your say," I told her. "Now let me have mine. I am a hunter. I hunt deer and elk here in Montana. We eat the meat. It's a way of life here in Montana, and I'm not ashamed of it. As far as trapping goes, I haven't trapped in years. Sold all my traps. Don't even own one anymore."

"Then what's the meaning of your e-mail address, 'Trappermike'? What kind of a disgusting name is that? If you don't trap anymore, why do you still call yourself a trapper?"

"It's just a name people around here know me by, Jewel," I wearily replied. "It's like they called that one character on *M.A.S.H.*—Trapper John."

"You have no idea how hard Timothy and I have fought here in California to ban trapping."

"As far as bear hunting goes," I continued, "I admit I have killed black bears here in Montana, and we ate the meat. Since my wife doesn't care to eat bear meat anymore, I've quit hunting them. Here in Montana, it's illegal to kill a bear and waste the meat. I go out now and just watch them."

"And what about all these books you've written? What's all this stuff about e-e-elk hunting?" she said, drawing out the *e*.

"It's a book I wrote to help bow hunters . . ."

"Oh my God! If there's anything worse than a gun hunter, it's a bow hunter."

This conversation was going nowhere fast, so I tried to steer the conversation toward Timothy Treadwell. "Jewel, what I really need is your help understanding Timothy's life. Like how you met, how you got involved in Grizzly People, how you . . ."

"I can't believe Roland even spoke to you. And Carol Dexter! I can't believe she spoke to you. She wouldn't even speak to the *Vanity Fair* people when they called." [*Vanity Fair* magazine had published an in-depth article about Timothy Treadwell's death.]

"Carol and I had a wonderful talk. I think it really helped her to know that someone wanted to know the good things about her son."

"Well, I just want you to know that I've phoned everyone and told them to watch out for you, to not give you an interview."

"Because I'm a hunter?" I asked.

"Yes, because you're a hunter. We have to be careful who we speak to. We don't want anything falling into the hands of people who aren't with us. I'm the one who should be writing a book about Timothy. I'm the one who knows him. But no, I'm spending all my time putting out fires with the f_____g press. In the meantime, people like you are making all the money using Timothy's name, and Grizzly People is barely staying afloat."

"Well, then you should write a book about Timothy," I urged her.

"I will, someday. I can't trust you people to give him an honest shake."

"Well, will you at least think about answering just a few questions about how you and Timothy met?"

"I don't know. I'll think about it. Good-bye."

I phoned Grizzly People three more times, but Jewel never returned my calls.*

---

*In an update to the Grizzly People Web site more than a year after Timothy's death, Jewel Palovak reiterated her belief that Timothy had protected bears from poachers: "Timothy believed protecting grizzlies from poaching was an integral part of his mission. On several occasions poachers threatened him, but during his time in Katmai, no grizzly was known to have been killed. In August 2004, nearly a year after his death, five bears were poached in Katmai National Park." Jewel clearly means to say that without Timothy's presence, bears would have fallen victim to poachers at Katmai.

In response to that update, a Katmai National Park investigating ranger told me: "There have in fact been incidents [in 2004] where bears were killed, but these animals were not killed in Katmai National Park. They were killed a long ways from Hallo Bay and Kaflia Bay [where Timothy camped]. . . . The State of Alaska [allows] limited hunting in the Preserve [Katmai National Preserve]. Those bears were killed out of hunting season on tundra in the Preserve area where legal hunting is allowed in season. They were *not* killed in Katmai National Park, and certainly not anywhere close to Timothy Treadwell's haunts." The perpetrators of those killings have been identified and apprehended, and charges have been brought against them.

CHAPTER 4

Adrenaline Junkies

> Whenever a client wounds a water buffalo, or lion, or leopard, and it holes up in the bush, it doesn't bother me a bit to go in there after it with a double-barreled shotgun loaded with slugs. Fact is, I like it. I've never felt more alive as when I'm crawling through the dense thorn trees after a dangerous wounded animal. At any moment he could be on me. What an adrenaline rush!
>
> —Angus Brown, Safari Outfitter, South Africa, 2001

ANGUS BROWN IS HONEST ABOUT his craving for adrenaline. Far too many people hide their lust for this high behind the rationale of research, or love for animals, or protection of animals, or understanding of animals, when, in fact, they just want to get eyeball close and feel the thrill scorch through their veins when the animal they're crowding finally turns and faces them.

Way back in 1958 shortly after our family bought our first television (in black and white of course), I turned on the new set just as the program *American Sportsman* began. The scene showed a silver-haired man in the jungle advancing cautiously through lush forest to a small opening where several dogs had a huge jaguar bayed. The instant the jaguar spotted the man, it sprang at his throat. While the cat was in mid-air, the man brought forth a spear and impaled it. The jaguar screamed and flailed at the air. It fell to the ground but sprang at the man again, and again was impaled by the spear.

I sat stunned as the jaguar, now noticeably slower, sprang twice more and met the spear in mid-air. Years later, I learned that the man was named Sasha Siemel. A native of Latvia, he had lived in Chicago before he emigrated to Brazil in 1915 and was hired to kill jaguars that were menacing ranchers' cattle. Bored with killing jaguars with a rifle, Sasha sought out a Tigrero—an Indian who hunted the deadly jaguar armed with only a spear.

Sasha Siemel's first hunt with a spear was almost his last—he was saved in the nick of time by a well-placed thrust of the Tigrero's spear—but Sasha was a quick learner and the next time was prepared for the jaguar to attack as soon as it spotted him. (This particularly aggressive behavior of jaguars is well known to circus trainers, who never use this species in their acts. Though smaller than lions and tigers, the jaguar can not be domesticated and will immediately spring at a trainer.)

Sasha Siemel became a legend as the news of his exploits reached an adventure-hungry public in the United States. He often spoke to adventure clubs in the States, but he delivered no poetic rhetoric to justify his deadly close-range encounters with 300-pound jaguars that did not shy away from a confrontation with a man. He admitted that he did it solely for the adrenaline rush. The episode I'd watched was filmed in the 1940s toward the end of his career. Sasha Siemel lived to the ripe old age of eighty and died in 1970 in Pennsylvania.

Adrenaline addiction in varying degrees is nothing new among active people. Most of us have it to a certain degree. We like the chemical response to danger and thrill; often, we seek it out. Of course, the majority of the pursuits of outdoor enthusiasts in search of an adrenaline rush (e.g., skydiving, bungee-jumping, hunting, fishing, car racing) are not inherently dangerous or fatal.

But with increasingly disturbing frequency, a new breed of adrenaline junkie, the animal-crazy eco-tourist, is making the news, and sometimes the obituaries. Recently, an enraged elephant in Namibia killed an American photographer when he moved in to take a picture of it. In Zambia a safari guide and a South African woman were killed by elephants. In Botswana a young American boy was dragged from his tent and eaten by hyenas. An American on his honeymoon was paddling a canoe on a river when a hippo rose up and cut him in half. And in southern Malawi's Okavango Delta, the crocodile population, protected by an agreement to limit the take of endangered species, has skyrocketed. Reports confirm that at least two people a day there are being eaten by the crocs.

It's enough to make a grizzly bear encounter seem tame in comparison. Actually, most bear viewing is quite safe because the majority of bear lovers are content to view a bear through a twenty-power telescope at long range. I recently accompanied a group of hikers with the Great Bear Foundation on a field trip to Glacier National Park to look for grizzlies. We finally spotted a bear about 500 yards away. Everyone was excited, but no one suggested that we slip forward and get closer. We were content to be in grizzly country and watch the bear feed on grass and glacier lilies.

For some travelers, though, that's not enough. The massive rush of adrenaline comes only when the encounter is close and the risk is great. Doug Peacock is a folk hero among the more rabid bear enthusiasts. In his book *Grizzly Years*, he relates several instances when he was charged by bears, but he is no advocate of moving so close to a bear that it feels stressed or threatened enough to charge. Still, he makes no bones about the adrenaline link between man and bear. "It's more than a rush," said Peacock in an April 2004 article in the magazine *Hooked on the Outdoors* in which he described encountering a grizzly up close. "It's a gift of life, a thing of beauty, and when you leave an encounter like that, you're living totally in the moment—it's as full as you're ever going to get."

One of the people that Doug Peacock sought to mentor about using restraint around grizzlies, for the good of the bear, was Timothy Treadwell. As with everyone else who tried to help him, Timothy agreed, often promising Doug that he was swearing off moving in on bears. He never did, however, as is evidenced by the videotape found in the camera at his campsite after his death. It showed Timothy advancing within 10 feet of adult male bears and females with cubs.

Timothy Treadwell wasn't the first man to push the envelope too far with bears. And he's not the first man to learn, too late, that a simple pursuit of an adrenaline rush with a bear can evolve into a fatal obsession in the blink of an eye.

A look at the newsstand reveals a plethora of slick adventure-oriented magazines for men and women, such as *Outside, Backpacker,* and *Camping World,* which appeal to people with money to spend on outdoor pursuits. The magazines feature articles about mountain climbing, kayaking, exploring—anything to get the blood pumping and the adrenaline flowing.

Polly Cavill, a wildlife technician with the U.S. Forest Service, told me she can easily identify with people today who are looking for new challenges. Her job monitoring infrared cameras that provide population and migration data on grizzly bears, Canadian lynx, and wolverines in northwest Montana's Lolo National Forest is never dull. "Adrenaline?" she asks with a laugh. "That started my first day on the job. I was carrying a big boom-box radio on my shoulder that contained a cassette tape of goshawk feeding calls. My job was to play the tape in certain areas to entice mature goshawks to respond.

"I was walking down this secluded forest road when I saw a big black bear amble across the road 60 yards away. Then I saw two cubs. I immediately started backing away, but the sow came at me on the run. Her ears were laid back, and she was popping her teeth. I yelled and waved my free arm, and she stopped maybe 10 feet away. Her hair was all puffed out, and she was gnashing her teeth. I knew the volume on the boom box was on high, so I slowly switched from tape to radio. Loud music belted out, and the sow jumped back and stood there looking confused and frightened. Then she ran back down the road, rounded up her cubs, and galloped into the forest. Oh yeah, there was lots of adrenaline flowing. I was shaking so bad I had to sit down. But I have to say that it was one of most thrilling experiences of my life."

Polly brushes a wisp of blond hair from her eyes and addresses the issue of Timothy Treadwell. "I've watched his career through the years, and it doesn't surprise me that he'd appeal to so many people. Our society today has subdued just about everything in the world except outer space and grizzly bears. If space is the last frontier, we've conquered enough of it to satisfy our curiosity and realize that it's actually a boring place.

"But grizzly bears? Now that's a whole different ball game. Even in today's age of cyberspace where computers rule the world, and we rule the computers, we've finally run into an animal that is bigger, faster, and stronger, and generally doesn't regard us as anything special. I think that grates on people—that there's an animal out there still unconquered. A last frontier, so to speak. And short of killing one with a gun, we have no choice but to either fear a grizzly or join it. I think that's how a lot of people who tend to be eco-warriors or New Agers feel about the grizzly. So when Timothy Treadwell comes along and tells us that the wildlife biologists have been wrong about grizzlies being dangerous, and that we can be friends with the grizzly, I think that appealed to a lot of people searching for something to get their adrenaline pumping."

No other group of outdoor enthusiasts pushes the envelope with bears more than wildlife photographers. I should know; I am one. I've had hundreds of wildlife photos, from the diminutive ermine to the mighty grizzly bear, published as inside and cover art in a variety of national magazines and books. So I can say with authority that when one peels away the poetic dialogue about artistic images, wildlife photography is all about adrenaline. Nothing compares to the excitement of focusing on a wild animal and "capturing" it on film, or "taking" its picture. With the regal bull elk, it's exciting; with a white-tailed doe, it's ho-hum; with a grizzly bear, it's an adrenaline rush far beyond anything even the hunter can claim. After a kill the hunter's adrenaline trip is essentially over, but for the wildlife photographer it's a rush every time he squeezes the shutter.

Timothy Treadwell, though totally inept at photography when he first began his forays into Katmai National Park, quickly became an accomplished photographer. Actually, most people can produce magazine-quality images—if they can get close enough. Powerful telephoto lenses in the 600 to 800 millimeter range help, but to get the really tight body and head shots that photo editors drool over, photographers still must advance to within 50 yards or less. With an elk it's not too risky. With a grizzly it's pushing the envelope. And sometimes photographers learn too late that they've pushed the envelope too far.

Montana resident Chuck Gibbs, an amateur photographer of some repute, was hiking along the southern edge of Glacier National Park with his wife when he spotted a female grizzly and her three cubs. Though Gibbs was aware that Bill Tesinsky, another amateur wildlife photographer from Montana had been killed when he pressured a smallish grizzly, Gibbs sent his wife back to the trailhead and went after the bears.

Chuck Gibbs was a great admirer of the grizzly. He believed the bears could sense this, and his respect for the bears would be reciprocated. He was wrong. When he didn't return to the trailhead, his wife alerted authorities, who found Gibbs's ravaged body lying among his photography equipment, which consisted of a relatively inadequate 400-millimeter telephoto lens.

Investigators are often at a loss to figure out such a tragedy, but this time they were able to accurately piece together the tragic chain of events when they developed the film in Gibbs's camera. The early frames show the female bear and her cubs at long range, feeding and appearing unconcerned. Succeeding frames showed the bear closer and closer, and the bear appearing more and more agitated. The last images, shot from about 50 yards away, show the bear staring back at Gibbs, then advancing toward the camera. Officials decided that the bear's life would be spared because she had been acting in defense of her cubs, and she had not fed on the body.

It is interesting to note that when park rangers arrived at the scene of the tragedy, they made a startling discovery—a .45-caliber unfired pistol in Chuck Gibbs's backpack. Despite a law prohibiting firearms in the park, and despite his spoken sentiment about a mutual respect between himself and the bears, Chuck Gibbs obviously felt some insecurity about his actions. Even illegally armed, however, he stayed true to his feelings of respect for the grizzly. He did not use his weapon, even though it cost him his life.

Unfortunately, there are far too many cases where photographers get their kicks and the bears pay the price. One Montana photographer was caught stashing grain and dog food behind his rural home that bordered Glacier National Park and taking photos of grizzlies when they came in to feed on the bait. Because there was no law against feeding bears, the photographer escaped punishment, but wildlife officials in that area estimate that upwards of a dozen grizzlies, habituated to human food near dwellings, were eventually destroyed. Montana has since enacted a law prohibiting the feeding of bears.

Feeding bears is a death sentence. Timothy Treadwell, to his credit, posted an appropriate notice on his Grizzly People Web site: "A fed bear is a dead bear." Tragically, it's sometimes not only the bear who dies. Such was the case with Michio Hoshino, a wildlife photographer who lived in Anchorage, Alaska, and lived to photograph bears. A native of Japan, Michio was a well-known personality in his native country and often hosted wildlife programs on Japanese nature channels.

In July of 1997 Michio arrived on Kamchatka Island in Russia's remote chain of Far East islands. The place was famous for its large population of brown bears that migrated to the Khakeetsin River rapids to feed on spawning salmon. Michio was guiding a Japanese nature film crew and was planning on doing some bear photography of his own.

But the group encountered an immediate problem. The summer salmon run was late, and the bears were hungry and roaming restlessly through the area, seeking food until the salmon appeared in the river. Some bears went hungry; other took matters into their own hands. The week before, a big adult male bear had broken into the single lodging cabin and ransacked the place.

Newly arrived photographers boarded up the windows and moved in. But with so many people and equipment in the tiny structure, the place was crowded, so Michio volunteered to sleep outside in his tent. Others warned him about the big bear, but Michio didn't want to leave the area because the salmon were due to arrive at any time.

For several nights the bear roamed through the area and tried unsuccessfully to break into the food cache. A Russian photographer tried to vanquish the bear with bear pepper spray, but the bear, perhaps having been sprayed in the past, knew enough to stay just out of range of the spray.

Unknown to the other men on the island, a Russian cameraman had arrived by helicopter and was observed luring the bear in with food. Disgruntled with the paltry food offerings, the bear broke out a window in the helicopter to get at the food inside.

Then the salmon arrived, and everyone forgot about the troublemaking bear. In fact, he was seen with other bears catching salmon in the rapids. But salmon must not have tasted as good as bacon or tuna fish, because one night the bear again went looking for human food. That night, the men in the cabin heard Michio Hoshino yell over and over again, "Tent! Bear! Tent! Bear!"

Several men dashed outside and saw Michio's tent being destroyed by the big bear. They yelled and threw things at him and banged pails with a shovel. The bear finally raised his head and looked at them, then picked up Michio's limp body in its jaws and carried it into the darkness. The next day a Russian hunter arrived and shot the bear. What was left of Michio's body was retrieved. By that time the Russian cameraman who had fed the bear was long gone, no doubt receiving accolades for his uncanny ability to get so close to a bear.

Anyone who believes that no one could possibly rival Timothy

Treadwell's controversial and dangerous actions around brown bears has never heard of Vitaly Nikolaenko, a Russian brown bear researcher who was so reckless that he surpassed Timothy in every way—to the point where Timothy's actions appear relatively responsible and considerate in comparison.

The diminutive sixty-six-year-old Nikolaenko had been taking risks a lot longer than Tim. He arrived on Russia's Kamchatka Peninsula (the same general area where Michio Hoshino was killed by a brown bear) in 1965, when Timothy Treadwell was only seven years old. Beginning in 1969, Nikolaenko was employed in the Kronotsky Reserve as a forest ranger and tourist guide, where he hiked almost 700 miles each year and averaged 800 bear contacts. Each evening he would return to his tiny one-room cabin and, squinting through the smoky light provided by a kerosene lantern, write down his bear experiences and observations in a series of diaries that would become one of the most important records of brown bear feeding, mating, and social habits ever recorded.

Vitaly had no formal education in wildlife biology. Instead, he was self-educated by persistently observing and filming the huge brown bears that roamed Kamchatka in abundance. His startling close-up photographs and videotapes of brown bears brought him the recognition he sought, but what he really sought was the closeness of brown bears, and he devoted his life to shortening the distance between bears and humans.

There is no doubt that Vitaly lived for the adrenaline rush of close-range encounters with bears, as evidenced by his penchant for seeking out the biggest adult male bears and dogging their moves. For ten years he studied a dominant male he named Karnaykhy, meaning bear with one broken ear. Then he followed another dominant male for eighteen years, even accompanying the bear to its den. He named this bear Dobrynya, meaning kind bear.

In the fall of 2003, Vitaly's diary noted that a big male brown bear arrived at a fishing spot near his cabin. The bear was a loner, choosing to fish in private and then tunnel into the dense alders to rest during midday. This bear was apparently not in tune with Vitaly's philosophy of bears and people living in close harmony. The situation did not set well with Vitaly. He began to confront the bear with his presence—a closeness that was not welcomed by the bear. Beginning in early December, Vitaly had several encounters with this bear, and he began carrying a shotgun because the male charged him twice while Vitaly was trying to approach him. One time he threw his backpack into the bear's face to save himself from an attack.

This last incident should have been enough to dissuade Vitaly from attempting any further approaches. Besides, the snow was getting deep and all the bears would soon be in their winter dens in the mountains above Nikolaenko's cabin. But this bear's behavior obviously rankled Vitaly. He was bothered that it wasn't acting the way he'd told the world that brown bears act—submissive and shy.

To his credit Vitaly was quite accurate in his assessment of the brown bear with respect to people. He wrote, "A bear instinctively fears man. This fear is another side of aggression. A bear has two alternatives—either to run away or to charge you. Most often the bear runs away. Bears prefer to avoid each other because if they choose to fight, they run the risk of injury. All bears, including dominant males, avoid humans." One of Vitaly's most controversial beliefs was that if a bear charges, you should run away because a bear does not see a man as his victim, so there is no reason to chase down a man. However, he was correct when he also proposed that the human is responsible for any human-bear accident.

But all those conclusions and musings were just for the rest of the world. Not far from those thoughts recorded in his diary was a big bear in Vitaly's backyard, and Vitaly was irresistibly drawn to it. One day he saw the bear resting on the snow. When Vitaly approached within about 80 feet of the bear, it stood and looked directly at him. Vitaly slowly circled the bear, though the animal demonstrated with aggressive posturings that he wanted to be left alone.

Vitaly wrote in his diary, "I followed the bear's tracks. Each time he displayed strong and loud jaw popping and lunged at me. He is vicious and dangerous. I could shoot him to defend my life, using [bear] pepper spray first if he attacks, and by shotgun if pepper spray is not effective." This statement indicates that Vitaly was fully aware that he was creating an atmosphere of very high stress for the bear. Yet Vitaly continued to pressure the bear for several more days.

On December 26, 2003, Vitaly followed the bear's tracks into the forest. The snow was now more than 3 feet deep, and the bear was sinking down to the ground, as evidenced by the huge furrow it had plowed as it tried to shake the persistent human harassing him from behind. Vitaly was on hunter skis, which kept him on top of the snow. When he moved close to the bear, it twice turned and lunged at Vitaly, but the deep snow discouraged its movement. Desperate to be left alone, the bear plunged into a dense alder thicket.

But Vitaly wouldn't quit, even though the bear was exhausted and Vitaly's actions were causing the animal to burn up critical body fat needed to carry it through hibernation. At this point Vitaly Niko-laenko should have backed off, if for no other reason than for the good of the bear. Instead, he abandoned all good sense and common decency toward an animal he was supposed to love and protect. Maybe he was thinking ahead to next year, and he wanted to leave the big bear with the memory that there could be only one dominant male in Nikolaenko's backyard, and he was going to prove that it wasn't the bear.

Vitaly was forced to remove his skis and wade through the deep snow while crawling under branches. He could see and hear the bear ahead at first, but then the tired, wet animal quit moving away. This was Vitaly's last chance to back away, but he wanted to "capture" the bear on film. With his camera in one hand and bear pepper spray in the other, he crawled forward.

The bear was only 5 yards away, but Vitaly could not get a good look at it. He bent down to slip under a branch when the bear sprang at him. The bear pummeled his head and chest with vicious swipes of its paws. Evidence in the snow showed the red coloring of bear pepper spray. Investigators could only guess that Vitaly didn't have the time or the room to spray the bear in the face before it was on him, or maybe he sprayed wildly as the bear savaged him. Another possibility is that the cold and snow inhibited the aerosol from leaving the can—a common problem with bear spray in cold weather. His broken, half-consumed body was found next to his smashed, bloody camera. The bear's tracks showed that after it had neutralized and fed on its tormentor, it bounded away through the snow and headed for the mountains to den up for the winter.

Timothy Treadwell and Amie Hueguenard had been killed barely two months earlier, and now fellow researchers were left to explain yet another tragedy. Why had Vitaly acted so recklessly? Why did he crawl into a thicket after a big, cornered male who was popping its jaws in a desperate warning that it wanted to be left alone? Some biologists who knew him explained that Vitaly's brash actions were nothing new for him. He believed that nothing bad could happen to him because he'd been in many bad situations in the past and the bear had always backed down.

Vitaly Nikolaenko believed that the bears allowed him to get close to them out of fear. Timothy Treadwell believed the bears' tolerance of him was an act of acceptance. Diverging opinions, but with converging results. The common thread between them was that they were inexorably drawn to get close to the bears. Remove that thread and both tragedies would have unraveled, and both men would be alive today. Instead they have left a lesson for the ages: Moving close to a bear for an adrenaline rush can turn into a fatal obsession.

CHAPTER 5

Bear Whisperers and Eco-Warriors: The Celebrity Factor

IN THE MOVIE *The Horse Whisperer*, Robert Redford plays a surly cowboy with a special gift of communicating with horses. The movie, an innocuous, feel-good film based on a best-selling novel, implied that it is possible for a man to possess a special metaphysical "gift" of communicating with an animal, which struck a cord among many bear lovers. In recent years a surprising number of people have stepped into the limelight by claiming that they have a special ability to communicate with bears. As Timothy Treadwell's close-range exploits with bears became more well known, the eco-naturalist crowd began to call him a "bear whisperer." In her eulogy of Timothy, Louisa Wilcox, Wild Bears Project Director for the Natural Resources Defense Council, wrote, "In a filmed scene of Timothy singing to a mother bear, flat on her back, with two cubs nursing on top of her, you imagined for a moment that she too enjoyed the song of gentleness. And you had no doubt that you were hearing a 'bear whisperer.'"

Joel Bennett, a wildlife filmmaker who lives in Juneau, Alaska, and who filmed Timothy many times, says, "I believe there are people in the world who have the ability to relate to wild animals in a special way and to some extent communicate with them. It's a concept that fits awkwardly in scientific constructs and makes biologists squirm, but I've seen Timothy do things that defy explanation. I've seen sow grizzlies bring their cubs over by him for safety while they leave to forage."

It sounds incredible, but Stephen Stringham, a bear behavior biologist and author of the book *Beauty Within the Beast*, says such behavior is no big deal. In his excellent video *Grizzlies Among the Glaciers*, Stringham mentions that it's not unusual for a female grizzly to leave her cubs close to him while she leaves to go for water or food. "I've also had sows come over by me just to get rid of a boar during mating season." But he's uncomfortable with the concept of a "bear whisperer."

The "bear whisperer" syndrome does more than make biologists squirm. It makes them scream, and it causes Center for Wildlife Information director Chuck Bartlebaugh to grouse, "Moving close to bears to prove that you can get away with it just leads to others trying the same thing, and it usually ends up tragically for the bear, and sometimes for the bear whisperer." While Timothy Treadwell became the most outspoken and visible proponent of a metaphysical bond between man and bear, other men also have clamored for the spotlight to show the world their special gift for getting close to bears without being attacked. An examination of some of these men may, by extension, shed some light on why Timothy Treadwell chose this controversial and dangerous path toward kinship with the bears.

Grizzly Adams may have been the first of the nationally known bear whisperers, although the term had not yet been coined in the 1850s when he first hit the entertainment circuit. A shocked buzz rippled through the New York City crowd when the famous woodsman marched his menagerie of wild animals down Broadway in 1856. In the lead wagon were three huge grizzly bears. The first two bears were kept in check only by chains Adams held in his hand, and he was astride the biggest bear! The man had a gift, murmured the spectators. And so began the American legend of Grizzly Adams, the country's first bear whisperer.

But Adams was no bear protector. He was a brutal butcher. In the summer of 1853 while on a hunt in Eastern Washington Territory (probably present-day Montana), Adams killed a female grizzly who had two cubs, then he chased down and captured the two cubs. Adams chained the female cub to a tree and muzzled her, and set about "taming" her. He attempted several advances without success. When the cub swatted his offered hand, he became enraged and relentlessly beat the baby bear with a cudgel until she was reduced to a cringing, whimpering, exhausted ball of fur. When he reached out to touch her, she did not protest, though she trembled in fear. Soon, he was stroking her and feeding her by hand. He named the cub Lady Washington. Before long the bear was allowed to roam around camp on a tether and eventually learned to follow Adams without a tether. On one of her first hunting trips with Adams, she assisted him in routing a female grizzly.

Lady Washington was also taught, after a series of intense beatings, to carry small pack loads on her back. Adams caused quite a stir when he strolled through the streets of Portland, Oregon, leading every sort of wild animal imaginable. This "California Menagerie" included such specimens as wolves, mountain lions, buffalo, and elk, and, of course, twenty or more grizzlies. Among them was Lady Washington, now weighing 300 pounds and walking docilely at Adams's side. Much to his pleasure, James Capen Adams was referred to thereafter as "Grizzly Adams."

Amazingly, while Adams was on a hunting trip to Utah, a Rocky Mountain grizzly visited Lady Washington for three nights while they were camped. The next year Lady Washington produced a single cub, which Adams named General Fremont.

In 1860 Adams teamed up with P. T. Barnum to produce a wild animal show, and Barnum, while commenting on the glorification of Adams, also noted his concerns about the man. He wrote, "His menagerie of California animals, captured in the wilds by himself, consisted of twenty or thirty immense grizzly bears, at the head of which was old Samson. Old Adams trained these monsters so that with him they were as docile as kittens, though in fact many were ferocious and would attack a stranger without hesitation. In fact, the training of these animals was no fool's play, as old Adams learned at a fearful cost, for the terrific blows, which he received from time to time, while teaching them docility, will ultimately cost him his life."

Barnum went on to explain his prophetic statement about Adams's demise. "During our meeting, Adams mentioned that his bears were getting the best of him and took off his fur cap and showed me the top of his head. His skull was literally broken in. It had on various occasions been struck by the fearful paws of his grizzly students. The last blow, from the bear called General Fremont who was always landing a bite here, a swat there, had lain open his brain so that its workings were plainly visible. Aghast, I remarked that such a dangerous wound would prove fatal."

On the morning of the show's opening, a band preceded Grizzly Adams as his menagerie passed down Broadway and up the Bowery. Of course, Adams stole the show, for he was dressed in an outrageous hunting costume at the head of the large parade of wagons. Three immense grizzlies were in the wagon with him, with Adams holding them in place with nothing more than hand-held chains. All the while, he was seated atop the biggest of the bears.

Doctors who examined his horrendous head wound doubted he could live more than a few days, but Grizzly Adams gritted his teeth and, though in intense pain, fulfilled his contract. Afterwards, he stumbled into bed and never got up from it. He died a few months later.

Though he had been immeasurably cruel to his bears when they wouldn't do, or couldn't understand, what he wanted, Grizzly Adams had preferred their company. Through the years, he had fallen into the habit of sleeping among them on a buffalo robe. But he was hardly a bear whisperer. Elephants, they say, have good memories. So do bears. Small wonder they ended up killing him.

Nearly 150 years passed before another self-styled naturalist/bear tamer came along to match Old Grizzly. It was in the mid-1990s that

Charlie Russell came on the scene in the beautiful landscape of Alberta, Canada. While some limelight seekers coyly shy away from that moniker, Charlie allowed *Backpacker* magazine to use the words "bear whisperer" in the caption for a photo of him very close to a brown bear on Kamchatka Peninsula.

Born on a ranch in southwest Alberta, Charlie is the son of noted nature writer Andy Russell and is himself the author of several books about brown bears, including the rare Kermode bear, a white-faced grizzly. Charlie's career as a bear whisperer began in 1994 while he was resting against a log in a rain forest along the coast of British Columbia. Suddenly, a female grizzly began stepping over the log he was sitting on. The bear moved closer and closer to the stunned Russell, until he could feel her breath against his face. For what seemed like an eternity, bear and man were face to face. Then the grizzly reached out and touched him with her paw. "It proved to me," he says, "that bears are not bloodthirsty killers."

Charlie Russell's search for the truth about grizzly bears and their behaviors led him to the Kamchatka Peninsula in Russia in 1999. There he and his partner, visual artist and photographer Maureen Enns, built a log cabin in a remote area that was filled with brown bears. On one walk alone he spotted twenty-five bears. But Charlie was frustrated because they all ran away.

That all changed in 1998 when he received a box from a zoo containing three orphaned brown bear cubs. Russell and Enns named the cubs Chico, Rosie, and Biscuit. They taught the young bears to fish and showed them edible plants to eat. When winter arrived Charlie expected to spend a long and enjoyable quiet season with the cubs, but they vanished during a snowstorm and denned on the mountain above.

Next spring, one of the cubs was killed by an adult male bear and the other one disappeared. Only Biscuit remained. Charlie Russell worked hard to habituate Biscuit and has been rewarded by the fame this bear has brought him. Numerous magazines and books have used the photos of Biscuit standing beside him while he fished, or Biscuit lazing on her back while Charlie stands over her in conversation.

But does this make Charlie Russell a bear whisperer? Dr. Charles Jonkel, one of the world's most respected bear experts and founder of the Great Bear Foundation, doesn't think so. "I wouldn't do that sort of thing because I don't want to create problems with the bears. You have to remember that Charlie is dealing with an orphaned cub he raised. The bears around his place are used to human contact. If he tried some of that stuff here in the Rocky Mountains, he'd get his block knocked off."

Russell responds to his old friend's criticism: "I'm not advocating anyone try this in Yellowstone. That would be foolish. I'm simply trying to show that peace between bear and man is possible."

To Russell's credit a PBS *Nature* program that featured him and Maureen handling the three orphaned cubs was excellent, as is their philosophy about the nonaggressive nature of most bears at Kamchatka. Unfortunately, while the spectacular scenery and the awesome bear footage were enough to carry this program, Charlie couldn't stay out of the picture. Toward the end of the program, he makes a point of venturing out alone and then advancing toward a small bear to show the audience that the bear is not afraid of him. But things start to get out of hand when the bear becomes stressed and retreats.

At that point bear and man should have separated. But Charlie advances, splashing his hand in the water while the narrator explains that Charlie is inviting the bear to play. The bear holes up 50 yards away and throws a fit, tearing at trees and rooting up brush as it puts on a display of bravado, which culminates with a hair-raising charge that the bear aborts at the last second. And then the narrator blithely states that with anyone but a person like Charlie, who has so much experience with bears, that charge could have been serious.

The Center for Wildlife Information reviewed this PBS *Nature* program and commented: "The National Park Service, Forest Service, Bureau of Land Management, state agencies and wildlife management agencies in Canada are all working to convince the public to

NOT do what Charlie [Russell] and Maureen Enns are doing. Russell's and Enns's actions are not safe for themselves or the bears. In the short term, they give a friendly up-close appearance to bear encounters, but when the public practices these activities, it results in dead bears, injured or dead people, and an increased fear of bears and bear encounters. Over and over again the leading causes of bear maulings are people's inappropriate actions around bears."

Russell carries bear pepper spray, but he says he has never used it. He further irritates bear experts when he expounds, "Those are things managers use to make bears hate people, though the word they use is fear. In my opinion a fearful bear is a dead bear."

Russell, uneducated in wildlife biology and unaffiliated with any sustained scientific bear research program, offers light responses when pressed about the danger of humans purposely moving close to bears. "I still think there is very little in a bear's nature that will make it turn on a human for no reason."

In ways similar to Timothy Treadwell, Charlie Russell seems to have enchanted more humans than bears. For a man with just a high school education, he's become more famous than his peers with their doctorates. Even otherwise serious journalists have fallen under his spell. In a *Backpacker* magazine feature on Charlie Russell, curiously titled "Touched by a Grizzly," writer Jeff Rennicke was provided with an extraordinary opportunity to put the bear-human issue in proper perspective. He might have chosen to share with the vast readership of this top-flight magazine the rules that bear experts suggest for proper behavior in bear country (which are largely opposite of Russell's approach). But Rennicke never called the Center for Wildlife Information to compare Russell's methods with the ones suggested by the pros. Instead, he gushed that Charlie Russell brought him close enough to Biscuit that she rubbed her nose against Rennicke's arm.

At the other end of the educational spectrum is Dr. Lynn Rogers, a wildlife biologist with a doctorate in animal behavior and thirty-four years in bear research. Also a renowned wildlife photographer, Rogers has had his work published in *National Geographic, National Wildlife* magazine, and many other prestigious, well-respected publications. In a video produced by *Animal Planet*, Lynn is introduced as "The Man Who Walks with Bears." The narrator of this television documentary announces that Lynn Rogers battles fear and myth to bring bears and man in harmony. This video is a joy to watch, with lots of close-ups of bears. The only problem is that Lynn Rogers is always in the picture with them. Even worse, he's always feeding them!

The story develops as Lynn seeks black bears to study around his Northwoods Research Center in northern Minnesota's Superior National Forest. But Lynn doesn't want to just study bears; he wants to be a part of their family, to have an intimate relationship with them. To that end he decides to put out feeding stations around his house and even on his back deck. Bear after bear is shown climbing the steps to get at food on his back deck.

Despite showing himself feeding bears on his deck and in the woods, and purposely advancing toward numerous bears, Lynn warns, "I don't recommend that anyone try this at home because it's taken me years to learn to read a bear's face and body language."

Throughout the *Animal Planet* video, Lynn is shown within a few feet of black bears, and he's always feeding them. They lick his hand, and you just know it's because there's some food residue on it. But even then, the bears let him know that they'd rather not have him so close: He tries to pet a female bear with cubs, and she bites his hand. Or he's kneeling beside a pool of water washing blood from a cut on his forehead, the result of a warning swat from a black bear. Lynn says, "She gave me a little whack to say, 'Back off. My cubs are coming down the tree and you're in my bed.'"

Lynn Rogers sighs and adds, "Sometimes . . . sometimes I just make a mistake." The narrator adds that close calls like this reinforce Lynn's warnings that nonexperts should not do what he does.

The video ends with Lynn kneeling at the mouth of a bear's den. He's feeding the female milk from a bottle while he takes one of her cubs from the den. Lynn triumphantly states, "From the reputation that mother bears have, everyone would say that I'm nuts, but the truth is that sows don't defend their cubs that much against people, and I do not worry about being attacked."

The Center for Wildlife Information assessed the biological content and message of the video and stated, "While many of our forests and parks are dedicating their resources to informing the public about the importance of NOT approaching, following, or feeding animals, especially bears, this video's presentation glamorizing a person who gets up close and personal to bears encourages dangerous or inappropriate actions by the public. Such actions [feeding, approaching, following] have led to the destruction of thousands of wild animals. They're also the leading cause of human-bear confrontations resulting in serious injury and sometimes death to both people and wild animals."

The report goes on to say, "Though the scenes of bears in this program are excellent, there are no messages regarding established bear avoidance and wildlife stewardship techniques, with the majority of the footage showing Lynn Rogers at an unsafe distance from bears, often petting and feeding them."

The Center for Wildlife Information doesn't care whether Lynn Rogers is a bear whisperer or not. They're more concerned with media misinformation that shows up-close and personal, face-to-face, hands-on interactions between bears and humans. "Look at me, I'm the center of attention next to the bear," they seem to say. "I am special."

The dangerous message conveyed by these "special" bear people is that other people might just decide to be special, too. These images lead more people to approach and interact with bears inappropriately. And, the Center notes, the Lynn Rogers segment is an example of inappropriate information received by the public regarding safety in bear country.

Credentials and experience are no guarantee that bear videographers and photographers will translate their adventures responsibly. In the opening scene of two grizzly bears fighting, in the program *Grizzly: Face to Face*, a British Broadcasting Company film narrator says, "Some people think grizzly bears are very dangerous, but not Canadian photographer and filmmaker Jeff Turner." The scene changes to a blond, bearded man filming a grizzly bear fishing within 20 feet of him. Working in some of the most remote wilderness areas of North America, Turner and his wife, Sue, have made more than a dozen award-winning wildlife films for such companies as the BBC and PBS. Among their many subjects have been buffalo, wolves, and bears. In *Grizzly: Face to Face*, the narrator goes on to explain, "Because Jeff Turner understands bears so well, he can get us closer to them than ever before. That's what makes this film so special."

While filming a female bear that he's known for thirteen years, Jeff Turner cements his place among the elite of the bear world with the statement: "I came to this place not knowing the grizzly, but there was something strangely compelling about getting close to such a powerful and dangerous predator. . . . It was a curious mix of fear and wonder that drew me to the bear. By allowing me in close, she's shown me the door into the world of the grizzly."

While not as outrageous or entertaining on film as Timothy Treadwell, Turner nonetheless advances toward a feeding grizzly while explaining to the viewer the best way to move in on one. Another scene shows a large bear moving toward him, while Turner explains, "In these protected areas during the salmon runs, you can slip right into their midst. In fact, I've been around hundreds of bears, and I'm impressed by their tolerance."

Makes you want to go out there and do the same thing, doesn't it? And that's the problem, cautions the Center for Wildlife Information. Advancing toward a bear is bad enough, but capturing the event on film and then, further, explaining how to do it can mislead someone into thinking they can have the same experience with the same success.

Is Jeff Turner a bear whisperer? He doesn't claim to be, but the

BBC isn't shy about making the claim that he has a special gift. What's frustrating about this entire program is that it would have been an excellent visual document about the grizzly—if the man had stayed a hundred yards from the bear and said, "I could sneak closer, but I'm not going to. I don't want to stress out the bear. Just because they're tolerant doesn't mean we should take advantage of them. That's why I have a telephoto lens." Now *that* would have been a great tribute to a great bear.

Jeff Turner, however misguided the Center for Wildlife Information thinks he is, can argue that his exceptional videography brings incredibly beautiful animals and landscapes into America's family rooms. Program host Jeff Corwin, on the other hand, cannot. Granted, he has been involved in habitat conservation projects since adolescence and has degrees in both biology and anthropology. He even has an honorary doctorate in public education. The question is how far has Corwin really progressed since adolescence in regard to his understanding of responsible public education. More importantly, do his films portray animals and their habitats accurately? On the *Going Wild* program and in a video by Disney Productions, he appears as a cross between Timothy Treadwell and crocodile hunter Steve Irwin. Anyone who hasn't seen this program *must* obtain a copy. It's that important to this issue of bear whisperers, misinformation, and the syndrome of the wannabe bear expert.

The program begins with Corwin dressed in a safari shirt and blue shorts, hopping among boulders and scrambling up hills while playing a cat-and-mouse game with a mountain lion. With the lion, on loan from Triple-D game farm and as docile as a house cat, in the background, Corwin explains in a hushed tone to the viewer the nature of this large predator.

Corwin takes a few steps and hears a fierce growling. He explains that he sees a wolverine, an animal you should never turn your back on because it is, pound for pound, the toughest animal in the world—although this one is another Triple-D resident.

Corwin then explains that he's in Glacier National Park seeking the mighty grizzly bear. He sets up a quick camp, then sets out—in the dark—to find a grizzly. We immediately hear a loud, ferocious growling, and the viewer expects a grizzly to pop onto the screen. Instead, with tremulous voice, Corwin informs us that the sound is the cry of a pine marten, a small member of the weasel family. While Corwin is shining a light on the poor little tyke, he explains that they are quite an aggressive animal, though a female marten tops the scales at about two pounds, while a very large male can almost hit three pounds.

Corwin gives up his search for the grizzly bear for the night and goes back to his tent, but a tremendous growling brings him back out. This time the cry is no small weasel. It is unmistakably a bear. Corwin goes forward with light in hand to find the mighty grizzly. He shines his light on BJ, a teenage grizzly (also on loan from the Triple-D game farm) nosing around for treats hidden beneath a log 20 yards away.

To his credit Corwin never claims to be a bear whisperer or to have a special relationship with them. He adds a boilerplate conservation message at the end of the program about saving the grizzly while extolling the virtues of Glacier National Park. Millions of young viewers undoubtedly have watched this Disney production. Corwin may not be, in this film, a grandstanding showman, but what is he teaching viewers about nature? My question is: What did they learn from this program? That an off-trail trek in the dark is the best way to see a grizzly bear in Glacier National Park? That the rarely observed pine marten, at under three pounds, is a threat? These questions reflect my opinion of the quality of this *Going Wild* program and the commitment Jeff Corwin made in it to accurately portray wild animals.

None of these men—filmmakers, photographers, naturalists, entertainers, or mere brutes—achieved the fame and notoriety of Timothy Treadwell. On the Discovery Channel's programs *Gentle Tim* and *Grizzly Diaries*, Timothy closes to within mere feet of several bears, cementing his reputation for outlandish behavior around grizzlies. Timothy's prime-time exposure spawned a spate of incidents, accidents, and citations issued to adventurous young men trying to achieve their own fifteen minutes of fame with the bear. Rangers in Yellowstone and nearby Shoshone National Forest tell of irate tourists who complain bitterly when rangers drag road-killed deer or elk away from roads because these visitors want to see a feeding wolf or a grizzly "up close." Bear-viewing guides in Yellowstone now tell of men and women showing up with Treadwell's book under their arms, along with a request to "get real close to the bears." Center for Wildlife Information executive director Chuck Bartlebaugh calls such actions "doing a Timothy." He told me, "I hear more and more stories about people 'doing a Timothy,' such as hiking off trails. The last two people that were killed by bears in Glacier were bushwhacking off trails where the bears hole up during the day."

THE BEAR WHISPERER'S SECRET

The question of how certain men are capable of repeatedly moving close to bears remains to be addressed. Is there, in fact, an aura, a demeanor, about men such as Jeff Turner, Charlie Russell, and Timothy Treadwell that somehow filters through the temperament of a wild grizzly bear and allows the bear to communicate love and trust? The one topic on which just about every knowledgeable bear person took exception to Timothy's exploits was his tendency toward anthropomorphism—giving human qualities to wild animals. His book, *Among Grizzlies*, is laced from beginning to end with the message: Humans can be friends with the bears.

Grizzly bears are wild animals—massive predators at the top of the food chain. They eat grass and plants as the main part of their diet but are always on the lookout for meat in the form of carrion or prey. It doesn't take someone with a doctorate in biology to figure out that a wild animal that lusts after high-protein flesh might look upon a human not as a friend but as prey. The factor that kept Timothy safe all those years was the instinctive fear that all wild animals, bears included, have toward humans.

Timothy didn't think it was fear. He thought it was love. He named "his" bears Booble and Ginger, Mr. Chocolate and Molly. He crooned, "I love you! I love you!" over and over to them and mistakenly believed that his words, rather than their instinctive fear of him, made them turn away, stopped them—sometimes—from charging him.

As his life among the bears continued, Timothy began mentioning that this particular bear or that bear sought him out for safety from other bears, or that female grizzlies herded their cubs to his side so they would be safe. But, as bear behavior biologist Stephen Stringham has observed, it is not unusual behavior for a bear to use a human as a shield. Timothy misinterpreted inconsequential bear movements. He may have even fabricated some. In either case he seemed determined to illustrate how grizzlies, rather than being simply wild animals, were instead caring, feeling creatures.

Even more troublesome was Tim's growing belief that the bears didn't just allow and accept his presence, but eventually came to seek it. After five summers in the Grizzly Sanctuary, Treadwell happened once again on the bear he described as his "old friend," Mr. Chocolate. In *Among Grizzlies* he writes, "I sat only thirty feet away, watching and photographing the entire event. Mr. Chocolate paused between bites and gazed up toward me, not concerned at all by my presence as he ate. We had certainly met under rather dubious circumstances on that day he caught me sleeping in his bear bed, yet throughout the years, Mr. Chocolate had not only tolerated my presence, but seemed to enjoy it."

In another passage in his book, Timothy further expounds on his belief that the bears welcomed his presence: "It would be quite interesting to know what the bears think I am; whether they consider me just another bear, an animal like Timmy the fox, or something altogether different. Whatever their evaluation, it is abundantly clear that most of the bears I live among either tolerate me, or enjoy my company."

Was Timothy truly blessed with some aura of love that the bears recognized? Or was his seeming invincibility more likely the result of highly tolerant people-conditioned bears with full bellies. The answer, known all along by bear experts and knowledgeable woodsmen, was that Timothy was dealing with a small and unique population of coastal grizzlies, whose domain comprises only about 5 percent of grizzly country.

In Southeast Alaska the grizzlies that live along the coast near salmon spawning streams tend to be less aggressive, due mainly to the fact that there is a huge abundance of food in the form of millions of salmon that migrate from the ocean up countless streams to spawn and die. Coastal grizzlies, called brown bears though they are the same species, grow much larger than their inland kin. It's not unusual for brown bears to weigh a thousand pounds or more. Some males weigh up to 1,500 pounds.

Like the snake charmer in India who allows his stunned audience to gape at the supposed magical power of his haunting flute music to charm into submission the deadly cobra slowly rising out of the basket within easy striking distance, Timothy Treadwell had a secret he kept to himself. The snake charmer's secret was that he'd previously forced open the cobra's mouth and snapped off its fangs, rendering the normally deadly serpent harmless. Timothy's ruse was that the bears he was dealing with on film, who were eating anywhere from forty to sixty pounds of salmon daily, mostly wanted to burp and eat and sleep. So when Timothy is shown on film walking by bears, those were bears who were often content to lie with bulging bellies and ignore him—a fact he knew about but failed to mention when he later basked in the attention his filmed exploits generated when he used them on television talk shows and news and nature programs.

Throughout the rest of grizzly country, the great bear remains a taciturn, surly loner—usually weighing less than 500 pounds. Always hungry, the inland grizzly is in a constant, desperate search for food to put on weight for the long period of winter hibernation. When a grizzly finds food, it jealously guards it, and sometimes you don't even have to blunder into it to get into trouble.

A good example of how even the coastal brown bear's actions can change when food is in short supply was shown in the Discovery Channel program *Grizzly Diaries*, which Timothy filmed and produced. While awaiting a heavy rain that would allow late-fall spawning salmon to run up a stream, the bears who are impatiently awaiting this glut of high-protein food to take them through hibernation begin to turn on each other, and several fights break out. Smaller and older bears stay out of the way of both dominant and sub-dominant males, lest they be killed and devoured. But when the rains come and salmon fill the stream, the bears again become seemingly good-natured and ignore each other while gorging on the multitudes of salmon.

Essentially, a bear whisperer approaches a bear repeatedly until the animal is assured that no danger is presented by the close approximation of the human. It's not a metaphysical gift. Anyone could potentially accomplish it, according to U.S. Fish and Wildlife bear expert Chris Servheen, but the danger to the human still exists. "Humans cannot read a bear's mind. Bears have all these social signals about their willingness to be passive or aggressive. To think that we could be a part of that is unwise at best." Unfortunately, the relatively placid nature of coastal brown bears during the salmon-spawning season was rarely mentioned aloud by Timothy Treadwell, nor by the news and nature programs he appeared on, leading millions of viewers (to say nothing of the children he addressed at schools) to believe that grizzly bears readily accept the nearby presence of nonthreatening humans.

Servheen adds, "Grizzly bears are wild animals, and they need be treated and respected as wild animals. We need to give them the space they need to go about their lives in the wild."

In support of Treadwell Jewel Palovak told the *Los Angeles Times* after Timothy's death that Timothy never encouraged others to do what he did. "He recognized that he had a special gift or was lucky," she said. "A lot of people said he shouldn't do what he was doing, or it was crazy. But he proved them wrong for a long, long time."

Chris Servheen counters, "Getting up close with a grizzly is no different than driving drunk. There are no lucky people. There are no 'special gifts.' There are only tragedies. Bears are wild animals, and we need to let them be wild. To do anything less is disrespectful to the animal and unsafe to both humans and bears."

Sterling Miller, senior wildlife biologist for the National Wildlife Federation, said, "Everyone who is really knowledgeable about bears has long had concerns about the message Timothy was giving to the public. Many years ago I told him that if he was injured or killed, a lot of bears would be killed as well, but he just wouldn't hear of it. He was very naive." A few years ago Miller published a paper documenting the upswing in bear deaths after someone is injured or killed by a bear. "Already game wardens in Alaska are hearing the fallout," Miller commented. "If Treadwell was attacked, people say, anyone could be attacked."

"It's not that bears are inherently dangerous, either," Miller adds. "Researchers routinely work safely in the presence of bears, but they respect the animals' needs and maintain an appropriate distance."

Despite Timothy Treadwell's death, the "bear whisperer" craze may not be over. Former Katmai National Park superintendent Deb Liggett, who dealt with Timothy over the years, informed me that Timothy's fame has resulted in several reports of other quasi-researchers in the park, operating without research permits and moving among bears in pursuit of their own agendas.

CHAPTER 6

Katmai National Park

IN KATMAI NATIONAL PARK, Timothy Treadwell played out his role as a bear whisperer in the presence of other humans—like bear-viewing guide John Rogers, who recalls his observations of Timothy in the park: "In the early days he wanted to maintain a secretive existence so he could blend in with the bears' habitat and within the bears' social structure. Sometimes when you come across a bear and it wants nothing to do with you, it will run off. As it runs off, it stops and looks back, runs and stops. That's all Timothy was doing, acting out a young bear, mimicking its behavior. It was actually quite entertaining."

Another bear-viewing guide who found Timothy entertaining was Bill Sims, a well-known pilot and hunting guide who also led bear-viewing tours into Katmai in the summer. One of Sims's favorite creatures was the blond "bear" that popped in and out of the trees, then loped up to Sims and introduced himself. Timothy would then turn to the tourists and launch into a protracted speech about the bears, often breaking out his phony Australian accent, especially when pretty women were present. Still, Sims liked Timothy, and he began preparing lunches for him whenever he brought tourists to view the bears at the Big Green, the vast sedge grass meadow at Hallo Bay that Timothy called the Grizzly Sanctuary.

But when Timothy expounded on the "love connection" between bear and man, Sims corrected him. Sims had seen too much of the other side of the big brown bears. "These bears just tolerate us," he'd correct Timothy. "They've only got one thing in mind, and that's to get as much food as possible in their bellies during the summer because they've got a long winter ahead. They're not here to be our friends."

In the face of such sentiment from a man who knew bears better than he, Timothy would fall silent, without an argument, preferring to wolf down the copious portions of fresh halibut Sims would invariably offer him. But if Timothy thought the sermon was over, he was mistaken. Bill Sims had something far more important to add. "Timothy," Sims told him every chance he got, "your love for these bears is going to get you in some serious trouble."

Timothy would merely shrug and reply, "If it happens, it happens."

Not everyone appreciated Timothy Treadwell's uninvited appearances. A good many bear-viewing guides brought back disturbing stories of Timothy screaming at them because they were bothering "his" bears. Other times he accused them of being poachers. He frightened some tourists by suddenly popping up, then scurrying away, leaving them unsure whether they were being harassed by a harmless eccentric or a dangerous madman.

While bear-viewing guides held varying opinions of Timothy Treadwell, bear biologists reacted almost totally negatively. Vic Barnes, who has since retired after seventeen years studying bears, was the leading brown bear researcher for the Kodiak National Wildlife Refuge when he encountered Timothy in 1990, long before Treadwell became famous. "The first time I saw Timothy Treadwell," Barnes recalls, "he pulls up in a skiff, and he's wearing shorts and hiking boots. When I asked him why he wasn't wearing hip waders, he answered that bears don't wear hip waders, and he wanted to do it like the bears did."

The relationship went downhill from there. One season, part of Barnes's research team observed Timothy engaging in bear-like behavior—splashing in streams, stooping over and running on all fours, and fleeing from visitors like a bear. Barnes pondered what he saw: "Treadwell claimed to be studying bears, but I really believe that he wished he could be a bear. What he was doing made absolutely no sense. It was contrary to any sort of research.

"Trained biologists try to stay out of view of the bears so as to observe them without bothering the bears. Treadwell did just the opposite, walking right up to certain bears that weren't dangerous and even camped among them. And each year he seemed to push it more and more, touching bears, letting a bear lick his hand, kissing a bear on the nose.

"It was stupid. Not only because it was dangerous, but also because it just made no sense based on what he said he was trying to accomplish. A couple times I sat him down and tried to patiently explain that he was contaminating his own research, if it could be called that. I explained that these weren't friendly, fun-loving bears; they were wild animals. I've watched them tear each other up, or just thrash an elderberry bush because they were having a bad day. If you fail to respect the bears as wild animals, you've lost your perspective. But he blew me off, said he didn't want to be lectured about the risks because he'd already concluded that he could handle the bears one way or another."

Barnes is among a handful of biologists who openly forecast Treadwell's death. He credits the tolerance of Katmai's bears for the fact that thirteen years passed before the risks Treadwell took ended in tragedy. Barnes remembers breathing a sigh of relief when he heard that Treadwell had left Kodiak Island after a few weeks and moved across Shelikof Strait to Katmai for his bear expeditions.

Not all biologists thought Timothy Treadwell was a total nut case, however. One of the few bear experts who initially supported Timothy's efforts was Larry Aumiller, longtime manager of the McNeil River State Game Sanctuary for the Alaska Department of Fish and Game. He once considered the possibility that Treadwell and a few other men might be capable of taking human-bear interaction to the next level of understanding, but ultimately Aumiller rejected the idea of humans and bears developing personal relationships. "I just don't think the bears give a rip," Aumiller finally concluded.

Dr. Stephen Stringham, Ph.D., a professional bear biologist and professor at the University of Alaska in Soldotna, is the author of a book detailing his raising of three orphaned black bear cubs (*Beauty Within the Beast: Kinship with Bears in the Alaska Wilderness*). No stranger to close range bear encounters, Dr. Stringham is the director of the Bear Communication & Co-Existence Research Program, founding director of the Bear Viewing Association, and president of WildWatch Consulting. Dr. Stringham said that he'd gone afield with Timothy a few times and never saw him approaching bears too closely. "He always stayed back a hundred yards when he was with me."

When Alaska Fish and Game bear biologist Sterling Miller first met Timothy Treadwell in Katmai, he was immediately concerned for Tim's safety. "Timothy knew very little about bears the first few years. He was really living under their graces. Initially, Timothy sought me out with questions about bears, but as his notoriety spread, and my criticism of him increased, he became less and less inclined to listen to me.

"I tried to approach Timothy from a different angle. I told him if he was injured or killed, a lot of bears would be killed as well, but he just scoffed. He was very naive. He actually thought that if he was killed by a bear, people would stash his bones out there and no one would have to deal with it." In fact, Miller published a professional paper documenting that whenever a bear injured or killed someone, there was a corresponding increase in bears "killed DLP" (in defense of life and property).

Miller went on: "I finally sent him a long, detailed letter pointing out the concerns I had about his actions, how those actions were being seen by the public, and how this could be detrimental to the bears if something should happen to him. He sent me back a really smug letter and summed it up by telling me that he would consider it an honor to end up as bear shit. When I read that, I thought, 'My goodness, what kind of person am I dealing with here?'"

A research wildlife biologist for the USGS Alaska Science Center, Tom Smith admits that he kept it light between himself and Timothy. It was Tom's way of trying to reach out to Timothy and maybe mentor him more as a friend. "It wasn't as if all us professional bear people stood back and waited for a bear to kill Timothy. A lot of us worked really hard to bring him around to proper behavior around bears. But as far as I know, no one ever reached him."

Dr. Stringham related that he urged Tim to be more scientific when he was in the field. "I told him that if he'd keep detailed notes on the bears he encountered, eventually other biologists would accept his work. I suggested that he keep track of sows and cubs, and what boars mated what sows, stuff like that which might lead to some tendency that hadn't been noticed yet. Unfortunately, he never followed up on it. One thing that did kind of irk me about Timothy was his tendency to use my ideas like they were his own. My specialty is bear body language, and I'd ask him if he ever saw a bear acting a certain way. He'd say no, and ask me what I thought it meant. I'd explain my idea, and the next week I'd hear about Timothy claiming that he'd discovered something about bear body language. It was exactly what I'd just told him."

When Deb Liggett became the superintendent at Katmai, she had been warned about Timothy. During our interview Deb told me, "I phoned Timothy at Grizzly People and told him I wanted to have a sit-down talk with him the next time he came to Katmai. In May of 1998 I picked him up at his hotel and drove him to a restaurant." Deb sized up the blond surfer-dude-type man who sat across from her. Even though he was 41 years old at the time, Deb found him to be kind of a big goofball, younger, it seemed, than his actual years. To Deb he also seemed rather harmless, even if his take on bears was extremely naive. "I laid it on the line to Timothy," Deb says. "I told him I couldn't have him harassing the wildlife, and if he didn't stop, I'd petition the park's solicitor to ban him for three years.

"That really got his attention. He had a scared look on his face.

We talked for over an hour, and he agreed to tone down his bear whisperer rhetoric. When I dropped him off at his hotel, I told him that I'd never forgive him if his actions caused one of my people to have to go out and harm a bear. He got so choked up he couldn't even speak. Tears rolled down his cheeks, and he just nodded. I really think my talk had some effect on him."

Any illusion that Deb Liggett harbored about Timothy Treadwell staying back from the Katmai bears was blown away when he appeared on the *Tom Snyder Show*. Film clips showed Timothy moving in very close to bears, and at one point he seems to bait a bear into coming to within a few feet of the camera for a salmon. "I screamed when I saw that show," Deb recalls. "I was appalled at what I saw, the way Timothy was behaving around those bears by moving in so close to them, and the very dangerous and inaccurate message he was spreading to the public. I got a copy of that program and took it to the Solicitor's Office at the park service's regional headquarters in Anchorage and told them that I wanted to cite Timothy for moving too close to the bears. I left the tape at his office, but the solicitor declined to recommend prosecution."

To her credit Liggett shrugged off this rebuke and tried another tack to bring Timothy Treadwell in line with proper bear behavior practices. She phoned Center for Wildlife Information director Chuck Bartlebaugh, and the Park Service enlisted him to talk to Treadwell about his irresponsible actions with the bears. Chuck and Timothy had already met when Chuck phoned him to protest his inappropriate behavior on television. As a result of Chuck's patient mentoring over the phone, Treadwell agreed to stop showing some of his closest-in film footage.

In spite of this small victory, Deb Liggett made it abundantly clear to Timothy that he was still in her doghouse. Timothy responded with a series of cordial notes and letters to Katmai officials—all females. These letters reveal a soft, sensitive, compliant—even needy—side of Timothy Treadwell. One letter begins: "I so-so-so want to thank you again for the wonderful meetings we had. I look forward to chatting with you on the telephone and in-person meetings."

In another letter addressed to Liggett, Treadwell pleads for mercy concerning a new park rule that required campers to move their site every seven days. The rule forced Timothy to purchase a motorized skiff to transport his camp. "I am a complete novice with a boat and motor," he writes, "and the seas here are frequently treacherous. While I will not give up my work in the wilderness, I fear for my safety as the season goes on and storms are sure to increase. On humanitarian grounds, I implore you to help me. Would it be possible for me to return to my inland campsite and stay there permanently so I can retire my boat? You could do this legally if you made me a volunteer helper while your people are not around."

In that same letter Timothy informs Liggett that he has made peace with one particularly troublesome bear-viewing contractor, and he then writes: "I am working hard to do my life's work correctly. *Dateline NBC* recently tried to rebroadcast the profile on me with an update. I stopped it. Many of my past critics from the bear science community are moderating on my work, even assisting and advising. [Timothy may be alluding here to Stephen Stringham's suggestion that he keep notes on his observations.] Once again, I humbly ask for your help and kindness: please let me return to my permanent campsite and retire my boat for the season." Liggett declined the request.

In another letter to Deb Liggett, he thanks her profusely for meeting with him over coffee, then moves on to the real purpose of his correspondence: "I understand that old tapes of my work have resurfaced on TV and that negative comments have found their way to you. This was old work that I did before you and I met and discussed the park's commercial standards that I now adhere to. I understand the pressures of your work and respect it greatly. I hope you will not punish me for this old work."

Liggett, still smarting from the solicitor's refusal to recommend prosecution after she'd furnished him a tape showing Treadwell virtually hugging the bears, replied with a very stern letter: "We have finished our summer season at Katmai National Park and wanted to take some time to discuss concerns we have over your activities and inappropriate behavior. We were alarmed by portions of a recent television special and the message that some of your actions portrayed. Specifically, we are referring to the shot of you touching a bear's nose and the general proximity that you had around the bears throughout the entire segment."

The letter spooked Treadwell, who was sufficiently concerned about his future in Katmai that he mounted a campaign to pressure Liggett to allow him to remain in the park. He enlisted the help of schoolchildren and teachers to whom he had spoken, and soon dozens of notes extolling Timothy's virtues flooded park headquarters in King Salmon, along with letters from several supporters. A February 15, 2001, letter from Louisa Wilcox of the Sierra Club read: "Timothy Treadwell has been enormously helpful in public educational efforts around grizzly bears." Wilcox then cites all the children's programs Timothy taught each year and ends with this appeal: "We hope his work will continue to the important protection mission of Katmai National Park, and to the overall health of the flora and fauna."

A March 2001 letter from the Greater Yellowstone Coalition states: "On behalf of our 8,000 members, I write you in support of Timothy Treadwell and the good work that he does for grizzly bears nationwide."

And on March 4, 2001, Liggett received a letter from a young lady named Amie Huguenard, who wrote: "The continuance of Timothy Treadwell's work is vital to the future of the Alaskan brown bear. . . . I believe individuals concerned with Timothy Treadwell's presence in Alaska don't have a comprehensive or accurate view of his work. . . . Restricting him from the park would be a travesty. It would injure not only the bears, but also the reputation of the park and its officials as he has a huge following of supporters. I urge you, with all due respect, to allow Timothy Treadwell to continue his important work."

Treadwell also embarked on a campaign to ingratiate himself with the Park Service. In the first of several letters to Deb Liggett in 2001, he writes, "I would like to propose an idea that could be of great service to you, the park, and the country. . . . I would ask to be a 'Bear Keeper.' I would keep an eye on the commercial bear viewers, keep weather statistics, teach the public bear safety, and be a witness for the animals. You would have my complete waiver of liability, and it would cost the government nothing." Alluding to the story that he sometimes told about being an orphan, he adds, "I have no next of kin that could litigate. . . . I am not personally wealthy. However, I am funded to do field work by some of America's wealthiest and most politically powerful families."

Ignoring the veiled implications of the last sentence in Treadwell's letter, Deb Liggett declined the offer because, frankly, rangers were still having problems with Timothy hovering too close to the bears. Despite the park's refusal, Timothy continued to send personal, handwritten letters to Liggett naming specific violations of commercial bear viewers: "I observed a certain group getting too close to the bears, and I took video of it and will send it to you if you like." He constantly reminded Liggett that "I observe and maintain all park rules."

Deb Liggett strongly suspected that Timothy Treadwell was doing nothing of the sort. And rightly so, as subsequent TV programs would attest. The TV segment that showed Timothy reaching out to touch a bear's nose should have been enough to have Timothy removed from the park. But Timothy was never cited by the park, despite the fact that he was often spotted stressing or harassing the bears by his close presence. One complaint submitted to the Park Service mentioned that Timothy was observed straddling a sleeping bear and photographing it.

One reason that Timothy stayed citation-free may have been the friendly relationships he enjoyed with some park rangers, occasionally socializing with them in the evening out in the bush or in Anchorage when traveling to and from Katmai. One female ranger told me, "I liked Timothy, and I considered him a friend. He was a great guy to have around the campfire."

There's a good reason that such fraternizing is discouraged. It's hard to have a good time with someone at night, then issue them a citation the next morning. And Timothy may have planned it that way. "Since then," the female ranger mentions, "I've learned that Timothy was not at all forthcoming with me about his actions around the bears."

Another female ranger in a supervisory position met with Timothy while he was en route to Katmai. "I flew from King Salmon to Anchorage and met Timothy there. We spent eight hours together, and I must say, he was the most extraordinary man I've ever met. He was so intense, so passionate about his work. He had so much energy. I sat mesmerized for hours listening to him."

Not surprisingly, this ranger never issued Timothy Treadwell a citation. Nor did any other female ranger. The citation Treadwell received for improper food storage had been issued by two male rangers. When I asked Center for Wildlife Information director Chuck Bartlebaugh about this matter, he commented, "Even with all the proof the Park Service had showing Tim moving close to bears on TV, he was never cited. In thirteen years of flaunting park rules prohibiting him from moving in too close to the bears, he was never cited. Isn't that proof enough that someone wasn't doing their job?"

When I queried the Solicitor's Office at the Park Service's regional headquarters in Anchorage about their refusal to take action in the Timothy Treadwell case, attorney Chris Bockman told me that he did not recall the particulars of the incident. Then he embarked on a lengthy explanation that the solicitor's office does not prosecute, per se, but investigates incidents and issues recommendations to the federal prosecuting attorney for, or against, prosecution. When I asked Bockman why the Park Service hadn't taken action against the television programs for showing Timothy Treadwell engaged in obviously illegal activities in Katmai, he informed me that he wasn't even supposed to be speaking to members of the press—or book writers—and referred me to park spokesman Paul Quinley.

But Paul Quinley couldn't quite recall the specifics of the Tread-well case, either. After I'd refreshed his memory, he struggled to explain the Park Service's non-action. "We just felt we had a weak case. The solicitor's office felt that the evidence against Timothy Treadwell was too weak because Timothy did not say on film that he was in Kat-mai. Besides, it appeared that Timothy was toning down his bear whis-perer rhetoric, and he cleaned up his Web site somewhat. We still weren't happy with his actions around the bears, and it remained a cause for concern with us."

Much of the blame for the Park Service's failure to control Timo-thy Treadwell has fallen on Deb Liggett's shoulders. But given the fact that the solicitor's office declined to recommend prosecution when shown irrefutable videotape evidence that Timothy had approached within mere feet of several bears in Katmai, it's understandable that Deb Liggett would throw her hands in the air and feel powerless when the next Treadwell television program aired.

The decision to not prosecute Timothy Treadwell is indeed a mystery to everyone except the legal arm of the Park Service. While Timothy had been careful to avoid specifically mentioning Katmai in any of his television programs or in his book, airplane flight logs of his trips in and out of Katmai were readily available. A ten-year-old could have built an airtight case, but the bureaucracy kept passing the buck between departments until the legal issue became moot and the field issues hopeless.

In interviews after Treadwell's death, Deb Liggett summed up the situation: "With Timothy Treadwell it really wasn't a matter of if; it was just a matter of when."

CHAPTER 7

Portrait of Amie

THE ENTIRE WORLD OF BEAR experts and enthusiasts knows that Timothy Treadwell was killed by a brown grizzly bear, and even a large percentage of the general public is aware of Timothy's rise and demise. In the weeks following his death, well-known personalities penned heartfelt eulogies to the memory of Timothy Treadwell. But almost nothing was written about the woman who lost her life with Timothy.

The official Web site of movie star Leonardo DiCaprio, who was a financial supporter of Timothy's, published a powerful memorial to Timothy, filled with accolades befitting a saint, but it never mentioned Amie, not once. Louisa Wilcox's wonderful eulogy on the Grizzly People Web site described Timothy as a luminary, larger than life, and likened him to famed animal researcher Jane Goodall, but she only mentioned Amie once, toward the end, along with the two grizzlies that died. I've kept track of the Grizzly People Web site; the same tribute to Timothy by Wilcox is still posted, as are other references to Timothy, but there are no other mentions of the pretty blond woman who went with Treadwell to the area around Kaflia Bay that Timothy called the Grizzly Maze.

To the general public and even, apparently, to many of Timothy's associates, Amie remains a paper figure in death, as in life, anonymous and nearly forgotten in the aura of Timothy's glow. But she was a human being. She was flesh and blood, with hopes and dreams—and fears—like the rest of us. And she had a family who loved her dearly.

Amie Huguenard, the "other person" who died up there in the Alaskan wilderness, was born in Valparaiso, Indiana. In high school Amie was well liked and could be engaging when necessary, but she normally tended to be on the quiet and shy side. And she was smart, graduating with honors that propelled her to the University of Colorado.

Valparaiso, Indiana, isn't exactly a nature lover's paradise. Its mellow oak and hickory hardwood forests turn a brilliant red and gold in fall, but they rarely stretch for more than a half mile before ending abruptly at some farm or freeway or parking lot or massive mall. Amie wasn't "into" nature early in her life. She was too caught up in the struggle for self-worth and personal identity that all teens experience through high school. Her diminutive size—she was barely 5 feet tall and weighed less than a hundred pounds—perhaps contributed to her shyness and introspective personality in her adolescent years.

But in college at the University of Colorado in Boulder, she blossomed. What mattered in college were results, and Amie excelled in college. It was during her college years that Amie discovered nature—and wilderness. She began to hike and bike, initially to ease the boredom and stress of college life. But Amie soon learned that the wilderness, with its quiet and unassuming presence, was in fact a powerful force that exerted its influence in a surprisingly potent, if subtle, way.

Amie had no interest in getting roaring drunk at frat parties and the string of college bars that ring the campus. Instead, she was off hiking. While other girls may have been experimenting with drunken sex and other humiliating coming-of-age experiences, Amie was finding herself in nature. And like everything else in life, when Amie found something she liked, she embraced it with zest.

After graduating from Colorado with a bachelor of science degree, Amie enrolled as a graduate student at the University of Alabama-Birmingham Medical School. While there, she hiked every mountain trail she could find. She traveled the length of the Great Smokies and

Timothy arrives for another summer among the bears via floatplane.

Timothy Treadwell.

Timothy sits reading as a
brown bear looks on.

Timothy Treadwell watching a bear
and her cubs as they learn to fish.

Timothy's trademark was moving in as close as
possible to giant brown bears.

Katmai National Park—the annual salmon run attracts dozens of bears to fish in its streams. And the bears attract tourists.

Timothy's interest in wild animals was not limited to bears.
Here he feeds a red fox he called "Timmy."

Fishing and feeding are summertime activities of brown bears.

Timothy was a guest on several talk shows, including *Late Night with David Letterman*.

Area near camp.
www.nps.gov/akso/images/
areanearcampsite.jpg

Closure signs posted.

www.nps.gov/akso/images/
closuresignsposted.jpg

Spot near campsite.
www.nps.gov/akso/images/
spotnearcampsite.jpg

Lake near campsite.
www.nps.gov/akso/images/
lakenearcampsite.jpg

The National Park Service temporarily closed off
the area of Timothy and Amie's campsite in Katmai
National Park during the investigation into their
deaths in October 2003. These pictures, taken at the
site by investigators, are posted on the Park Service
Web site. To view these images full size, go to the
Web address provided below each image.

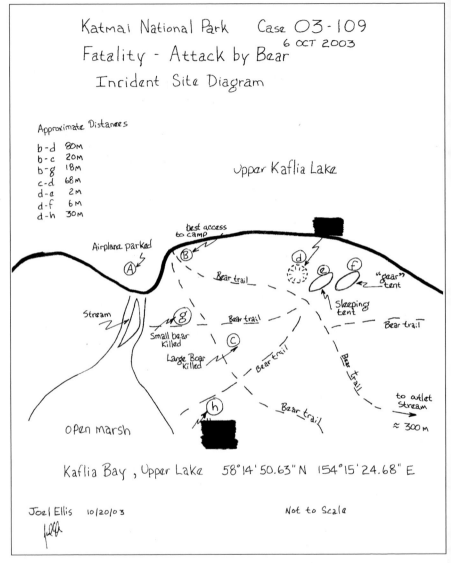

National Park Service incident site diagram.

even hiked through the remote wilderness in New York's Adirondack Mountains.

The eastern mountains were enjoyable, but Amie yearned for Colorado's Rocky Mountains. For in that state was a wilderness so vast that only the mighty state of Alaska eclipsed it.

With a masters in molecular biology, Amie was faced with a conundrum. To expect any kind of career in that field required a doctorate. But she was tired of school. She wanted to get out in the world and work at a job and explore nature on the weekends. She returned to Boulder and worked at a variety of jobs in the medical profession, her degrees aiding her in obtaining decent positions but keeping her from rising to the top of the professional medical field. That was okay with Amie; her interests had changed. The natural world drew her spirit like a magnet.

Already lean and muscular, Amie became a health and fitness devotee. She hiked, she biked, she ran. Even after an exhausting double work shift, she'd run—in the heat of summer, in winter over frozen ground and ice in the dark. Those who knew her swore that there wasn't another woman in the world any tougher, pound for pound, than Amie. Her stamina was amazing; she'd carry enormous loads on her back that most men couldn't handle.

On weekends she began to explore the endless snowcapped Rocky Mountains. She visited Rocky Mountain National Park and exulted in the startling visual delight of Alpine Village—where the high country was carpeted with velvet alpine meadows and wildflowers as far as the eyes could see. She witnessed the beauty of the bull elk, their massive antlers covered in velvet, who roamed peacefully, oblivious to the human visitors. She also hiked extensively through Utah's pristine Wasatch Mountains.

One summer she hiked throughout the Grand Tetons, and it was there that she first felt the presence of an animal so great and so terrible that it forced her to change the way she hiked and the way she thought. This was grizzly country, and in this place the great bear reigned supreme. She adapted; she became more careful. Her experience in the Tetons would prove useful in the future.

While Amie's basic personality tended to be somewhat introverted on first meeting, she could be rather animated with her friends, and her voice resonated above the din of others when she felt moved or excited about an issue. And nothing got Amie excited like nature. She became a passionate animal lover and supported a variety of causes. In the medical complex where she worked, one osteopath said he could always get a rise out of Amie by teasing her about wilderness or baby seals. Amie would respond with lighthearted replies, but she always made sure they knew her heart when she turned serious at the end of the jest-fest and commented, "They're very important to me, you know."

All of nature interested her, but she was especially intrigued by the grizzly. Here was an animal that had been hunted, trapped, and poisoned to near extinction, yet it persevered. The great bear preferred to avoid humans, but when provoked would resist unto death. Here was an animal with heart, and with resolve. Amie read every piece of literature she could find on grizzlies. One day in 1999 at a bookstore she came across a volume titled *Among Grizzlies*. She read the entire book in one sitting, captivated not only by the outer struggle the author experienced living among wild grizzlies in the Alaska wilderness but also by the inner struggle he fought with the demons of drugs and alcohol.

A few months after she'd read the book, Amie heard of an upcoming talk by its author in Boulder and made plans to attend. Though vitally interested, Amie took a seat in the back of the auditorium where she missed nothing. She was mesmerized by the fantastic Alaskan scenery and the bears. But as the program continued, she became more and more distracted by the tall, blond, handsome speaker himself. Timothy Treadwell's dashing, hyper, passionate delivery left her spellbound. At some point she stopped studying the video screen that showed scene after scene of Timothy approaching within mere feet of bears. Instead, she began studying the man who was in perpetual motion even while the video was running. After the seminar ended and the applause died down, she attempted to go forward and shake the man's hand, but a crowd of female admirers thronged the man named Timothy Treadwell, and she headed home.

But she couldn't get him out of her head. In January 2000 she wrote him a formal letter that began, "Dear Mr. Treadwell, I had the pleasure of attending one of your presentations and want to inform you how much I enjoyed it."

Long before Timothy Treadwell loved bears, he loved women, and he was not averse to using his newfound fame to his advantage in this area. Amie had enclosed her phone number, just in case Timothy ever wanted to talk about bears. One day he did in fact pick up the phone and dialed Amie's number. They enjoyed a long conversation, then another and another. At this point in Timothy's career, he needed a telephone and address book to keep track of his many admirers. To remind himself of the person behind the names, Timothy was in the habit of adding a few words beside each name to prompt his memory. Beside Amie's listing he penciled in: "Great person, good heart."

During the next winter when Timothy again made a speaking tour through Colorado, he and Amie met. Timothy Treadwell was unlike any other man she knew. The doctors she associated with in professional circles tended to be stiff and ego-driven and concerned with the world as they saw it. Timothy was different. His world revolved around wild animals, especially the bears he referred to as "his."

As with everything else in her life, after she met Timothy Treadwell, Amie gave herself totally to him—physically, emotionally, spiritually. What began as a friendship evolved into love. Reflecting on her sister's feelings about Timothy, Kathleen Huguenard Stowell quotes a note she received from Amie: "Because of obstacles and logistics, most people are too afraid to follow their heart, but those people who do are courageous and inspiring." Kathleen shared her thoughts on the relationship, as filtered through Amie: "They were bonded together on a totally unique level. Amie and Timothy were doing what their hearts told them to do. There could be no other way for them."

But nothing about Timothy Treadwell was ordinary, from his relationships with bears to his relationship with Amie. She wanted something permanent, and she let him know that. "I think you are amazing," he responded, "but I'm not really the settling-down type. It's just the way I am, and I won't change."

Many women would have gone home and had a good cry, but not Amie. "Tim's not a family guy," she told a friend. "He is who he is."

One aspect of his personality that Timothy was truthful about was his tendency to maintain some emotional distance in relationships. While his friends and peers were at an age when they were settling down, Tim headed in the opposite direction. "I don't want any little ones running around," he repeatedly told one of his female friends in Kodiak. He'd had enough tumultuous relationships with women, and he'd always ended up unattached and heading back to the bears, who never disappointed, or judged, or tried to change him.

Timothy's relationship with Amie was officially a friendship, but behind the scenes they fell somewhere in between lovers and friends. Treadwell would pull away, then come back. Back and forth, up and down, hot and cold, and always with a tendency toward the dramatic.

However fickle Timothy may have been, Amie remained rock solid. When Timothy contracted giardiasis at Kaflia Bay (the site of Timothy's Grizzly Maze), acquiring the intestinal parasite from drinking water contaminated with beaver feces, his temperature shot up to 104 degrees, producing hallucinations during which he thought he saw Amie walking by the front of his tent. He made an urgent phone call to Palovak and Huguenard with his satellite phone. Amie express-mailed medicine to Kodiak, and a bush plane dropped the medicine at his camp.

Prompted by desperate personal loneliness and a growing affection for Amie, Timothy invited her to join him in Alaska in 2001 for a couple of weeks. Timothy would later write that the visit deepened but complicated their relationship. During this visit Timothy discovered another side to Amie. Physically, she was tough as nails. Though barely half his size, she could out-pack, out-walk, and out-tough him.

That summer the bears were a little nervous and testy at Hallo Bay, also known as the Big Green. But with Amie there Timothy was a lot more careful. He never approached the bears, but instead allowed the animals to move toward him. He and Amie would stand perfectly still, and Timothy would whisper instructions to Amie as he sang love songs to the bears. For the most part Timothy made sure they stayed away from the big males. Only once did they have a problem, when a big male forced them to back off by growling menacingly.

The quiet of the Alaskan bush suited Amie. "It's like heaven up there," she told her friend Kim Sullivan, who worked with her. "You haven't lived until you've bathed in a river with bears." Another time she related to Sullivan how she and Treadwell were trying to wade a river when a big brown bear chased them back. "It was a two-hour standoff, and at times the bear got so close I could feel his breath in my face."

Amie visited Timothy in Alaska again during the summer of 2002. Their relationship hadn't solidified any more, but neither had it deteriorated. Amie accepted the fact that, at least for the time being, Timothy would always have the wanderlust, that he would always have another love in his life, and that her interests would always come second to his "research." But at least on her part, she'd made an emotional commitment, and until that "something" within her spirit changed, she would remain faithful.

However, events occurred during the winter of 2002 that would either make or break their relationship. Back in California Timothy agreed to allow Amie to move in with him, and the masthead for *Grizzly People News* listed Amie as the organization's "Expedition Coordinator and Consultant." In the spring of 2003, the year she turned thirty-seven years old, she began making arrangements to move to California. She visited Timothy in Alaska for a few weeks in July 2003, and when she returned home, she quit her job in Colorado and began searching for a new position in the medical field near Tim's Malibu apartment. She landed a job as a physician's assistant at Los Angeles's prestigious Cedars-Sinai Medical Center, assisting a neurosurgeon who specialized in head trauma. When Timothy returned in the fall from his brutal Alaskan pilgrimage (a long stay in the Alaskan bush is tough and demanding), they planned to live together.

So far, the relationship between Amie Huguenard and Timothy Treadwell had always been on his terms, but with the decision to move in together, Amie most certainly would expect a mutual reciprocation of emotional commitment—from a man who had all along made it clear that he was not the settling-down type.

Timothy may have been on the cusp of exploring a new phase in his life—a monogamous one. And maybe not. Joel Bennett, a friend and filmmaker who'd made three films with Timothy, had been working with him on another film just weeks before his death. Bennett was surprised to learn at the memorial service that Amie Huguenard had been Timothy's girlfriend.

Chuck Bartlebaugh met Amie twice in 2001 during a grizzly bear symposium in Boulder, Colorado, just a few months before her first trip to Alaska. Both times she was with Timothy. "She was real quiet and reserved, like she deferred to Timothy to do all the talking," Chuck remembers, then struggled to find the right words to describe Amie. "She was just so special. She reminded me of a little princess. She was so petite, so glowing, so . . . ethereal. At the time I had some serious issues with the way Timothy was behaving around bears, and I was concerned about Amie. You could tell from the look in her eyes that she believed every word Timothy said as gospel. She was one of those trusting kinds of people, the type who always thought the best of everyone. If he said it was safe to be around bears, then it must be true. If some rich people were giving him money to do it, then it must be all right. If the Park Service was allowing Timothy to do those things up there, then everything must be okay."

A hard look comes to Chuck's face when he says, "A lot of people in the Treadwell camp brush off her death by saying that Amie knew what the risks were, but there's no way she could have known what she was getting herself into up there. And I think Timothy knew it, too. That's why he kept her going up there a secret."

It's still very painful for Amie Huguenard's family to speak about her death. Her sister Kathleen initially spoke to the press about her sister, but she became distraught over probing phone calls by the press and arranged for an unlisted phone number.

Amie's mother, Marilyn, is still in mourning. She is devastated by the loss of a daughter she calls a "wonderful, wonderful person." Marilyn has steadfastly refused to speak to the press about her daughter, but she agreed to speak to me as long as we didn't broach the personal aspects of Amie's life. "Our family is just devastated about losing Amie," she told me. "It was such a tragic and senseless death. We have no good feeling about it, no explanation that satisfies us. It has left a gaping hole in my life. I'm working my way through it, but it's going to take a long, long time."

For Marilyn, at the time of my interview with her just six months after Amie's death, the pain was still too fresh, too vivid. To speak of her lost daughter put her in danger of inviting back the savage onslaught of searing pain that slices through her heart. It is a very private, maddening agony that only a mother who has lost a child in such a manner would understand. Someone like Timothy's mother, Carol Dexter.

CHAPTER 8

The Timothy Treadwell No One Knew

Treadwell's supposed claims of research were nothing more than his own private Jackass show, minus the cart.
                                        —Wildlife Biologist

Do those people who say terrible things about my Timmy know how much it hurts me to hear people talk like that?
                                        —Carol Dexter,
                                        Timothy Treadwell's mother

PUTS A DIFFERENT SPIN ON IT, doesn't it? A mother's love for a lost son. Something for every harsh critic to consider before he expounds upon the imperfections of a dead man. No matter how manipulative or wrong or misguided he is made out to be, Timothy Treadwell was someone's son, brother, friend.

My own opinions were tempered during an emotional, hour-long phone conversation with Carol Dexter, who graciously helped me fill in the voids and dispel some of the misinformation swirling about in the press since his death. In turn, she was also very thankful (and pleasantly surprised) that someone would seek from her the truth about her son.

The first fact Carol Dexter wanted to clear up was the supposed estrangement between Timothy Treadwell and his family. "Timmy called us at least four times a year," Carol said, pride and joy evident in her voice. "It was so wonderful hearing about all the exciting things he'd done since our last talk. But we didn't just talk about bears. We'd chat about his girlfriends, about the movies. We're all movie fans, and we'd talk for hours about the littlest scene in a new movie."

Carol's voice grew husky with emotion when she commented, "Tell them that my Timmy was a wonderful son. Not at all like they made him out to be. He was caring and kind. He loved animals. Oh, how he loved animals! We always had cats around the house, and for the longest time we had a pet duck. Then one day Timmy and his brother rescued two baby squirrels and brought them home. One died, but Timmy and I nursed the other squirrel. That squirrel and Timmy really bonded.

"We kept it in the cellar and Timmy would play with it. He'd pull a sock attached to a string and the squirrel would chase it. This went on for hours. And this squirrel only liked people with blond hair. It bit anyone with dark hair. Timmy and I have blond hair, so it liked us. It even bit Valentine [Timothy's dad]. Then one day it bit a neighbor kid and they called the wildlife welfare people, and they made us take the squirrel back to the woods and release it. I remember how Timmy cried when we let it go. He watched for days, hoping that squirrel would come back."

When I read Timothy Treadwell's book, his reminiscence about a troubled childhood lost in fantasies and hyperactivity prompted me to wonder if Timothy didn't suffer from depression or ADD (attention deficit disorder). When I asked his mother about those possibilities, she commented, "Back in those days kids weren't checked for that kind of stuff. We just knew that Timmy was always a dreamer, and it was hard keeping him paying attention. But now that I think about it, yes, I can see that he might have had ADD. I do know that he was dyslexic. He wanted to read his words backwards. And, of course, he was always hyper, always bouncing off the walls, always in motion.

"But he was a good kid, not a problem child at all. He was just a joy to have around because he was always into something, always had something on his mind, some wild ideas about birds or squirrels. He had a paper route, and he loved the Fourth of July because of all the fireworks. He loved shooting off fireworks. We lived close to the ocean, and Timmy had his own boat. He'd go fishing and crabbing and exploring. And he was a fighter. He was always getting into scraps.

"And he just loved nature. I remember the first Arbor Day when Timmy was in sixth grade. His class marched 4 miles to a lake and cleaned the place up. It doesn't surprise me that he eventually turned back to his nature roots with the bears. He just adored animals. He went a couple times to Nova Scotia to protect the baby seals from getting clubbed to death. Toward the end he seemed as interested in helping there as he was with the bears. Now, I wish he had."

Carol's voice rises. "Toward the end there were so many people criticizing his every move. They crucified him because he went on the *David Letterman Show* and said that grizzly bears were party animals. People said he was making bears out to be friendly, fun-loving animals, but Timmy told me he meant that they were always in a party mood to eat and eat and lay around and get fat and happy."

In his book, *Among Grizzlies*, Timothy mentioned that as a child he dreamed of being a mighty grizzly bear. His mother confirmed that fascination. "Little Timmy's favorite cuddly doll was a teddy bear, and when he grew out of the baby stage, he kept his teddy bear in his room and even took it to California with him." There is a pause on the other end of the phone line while Carol collects herself, then speaks in a soft voice, "Jewel Palovak sent me his teddy bear after he died. It's on my bed now, one of my most prized possessions."

In high school at Connetquot High School in Bohemia, New York, Timothy joined the swim team and excelled, but fellow swimmer and friend George Neyssen remembers Timothy Treadwell as kind of a party guy with few friends. "His personality was such that you couldn't really get close to him because he would go off on people. I can't even recall him having a girlfriend back then."

Though dyslexic, hyperactive, and possibly ADD, Timothy Treadwell got good enough grades, and he excelled in athletics. He received a partial college scholarship to Bradley University in Peoria, Illinois, where he set a diving record in the three-meter springboard. Timothy's main competition was fellow diver Jeff Martin. "He was kind of feisty," Martin recalls. "Always ready to fight over the smallest thing. One time he came after me, and the coach had to break it up. I was quite a bit bigger, so I just fended him off."

Bradley officials won't divulge why Timothy left the diving team after two years and eventually dropped out of school. "I don't remember Tim having any friends," Martin recalls. "I think it was because he was a bit of a storyteller. He exaggerated a lot to get people's attention."

After returning home to New York, Timothy got drunk one night, wrecked the family car, and ended up in jail on a DUI charge. Though his parents steadfastly maintain that Timothy was not the hellion he claimed to be, one gathers from his journals that Treadwell considered himself somewhat of a lost cause. The wreck of the family car while he was intoxicated no doubt served to confirm his already low opinion of himself, and he decided to move to California in 1977 to begin his life anew. He spent his first seven months living in Venice with his older sister until he could afford his own apartment.

Timothy took a job as a waiter on the luxury ocean liner, the RHS *Queen Mary*, then owned by the City of Long Beach and operated as a restaurant. When his father and mother, Val and Carol Dexter, came out to visit a few years later, Timothy proudly took them on a tour of the boat. However, Carol recalls that she was concerned about Timmy. "He seemed somewhat adrift and restless. He still smiled a lot, but I could tell that he was unhappy about his plight in life. Timmy was always such a dreamer. He always wanted to be someone else, do something no one else would think of doing, something out of the ordinary."

It was during this period that Timothy legally changed his name to Treadwell from Dexter. He told some people that the name change was to help him start a new life when he moved to California. Timothy claimed at various times that the "Treadwell" name came from a stage name he'd used during a school play. He told others it was his mother's maiden name, and still others that it was a name he'd taken from his English ancestry.

From 1979 to 1987 Timothy Treadwell worked a succession of bartending jobs, and according to him it was in this dark, late-night atmosphere that he began experimenting with drugs. He claims that a fight at a drug party ended with a drug dealer pointing a gun at his head. Timothy wrote in his account of the event that he screamed at the man, "Kill me . . . ," but as the neighborhood lights flicked on, the dealer declined, walking away from Treadwell shaking his head. Shortly after that evening, Timothy alleges, a drug overdose almost claimed his life, and that was the catalyst that sent him into the wilds of Alaska to cleanse his life.

Regardless of what people may have thought of his behavior around bears, they had to hand it to the guy. He pulled himself out of the drug sewer and tried to make a difference in the world. A fantastic success story.

Maybe too fantastic. Some of his friends in California don't remember it that way at all. Ira Meyer met Treadwell in the Malibu area in the late 1980s and said he never knew Timothy to be a drug user. Others who knew him back then say he was clean and sober. Karyn Kline, a former Californian now living in Washington State says she met Treadwell in Sunset Beach in 1981. "He had this Cockney accent," recalls Kline. "He told my brothers that he was an orphan from England. He said he'd been thrown out onto the streets by his parents, so he headed for America. My family at first took him in because they felt sorry for him." Eventually, according to Kline, the family sort of caught on to him. "He was always getting into fights," she adds. "He finally left town when he heard several people were out to get him. They may have been drug dealers, but I'm not sure."

The Kline family lost track of Treadwell until 1997. "After he published that book," Karyn mentions, "he came back to Sunset Beach and tried to brag to my dad that he finally made the big time. I think his whole thing was to be somebody. He was quite a character. He probably should have been an actor. I'm amazed that he got his life together."

The book that Karyn Kline is talking about is, of course, *Among Grizzlies*, the chronicle of Timothy Treadwell's life after he left California for the wilds of Alaska. A narrative of his first six seasons in Alaska, the book is an impassioned account of the rededication of his new life to understanding the grizzly bear and saving the bears on the Alaskan coast from poachers.

I find the book to be both fascinating and troubling. I love bears, especially grizzly bears, and being something of a knowledgeable grizzly person myself, I was particularly bothered by Timothy's insistence on continually getting close to the bears, often at great risk, and his perplexing resolve to save the bears from poachers, though he never mentioned or photographed bear carcasses. I read the book three times, hoping the disquieting feeling would cease, but it didn't. I couldn't explain exactly why, but I felt that there was a lot more to the Timothy Treadwell story.

After I spoke with Timothy's mother, Carol Dexter, I called Colorado resident Roland Dixon, Timothy's chief financial backer. Two weeks before our phone conversation, I'd sent Dixon one of my bear books, *True Stories of Bear Attacks: Who Survived and Why*, along with a letter of introduction explaining this book project. Dixon asked why I was writing a book about Timothy Treadwell, and I explained that, in my opinion, the people for and against Timothy Treadwell were so polarized that someone needed to write a fair and accurate book about his life. Following a long silence, Roland asked in a quiet voice, "What do you want to know?"

"For starters," I replied, "how did you meet Timothy?"

Roland began to speak, and he didn't stop for an hour. "I met Timothy through Charlie Russell. Charlie told me about Tim's work, so I called [him] and we hit it off. I liked what Tim was doing, saving the bears from poaching and showing people that bears aren't killers. In my opinion he was a true bear whisperer. How else could the guy get within 2 feet of a sow grizzly nursing her cubs? The guy just had something the rest of us didn't have. He could blend right in with the bears. I mean, he lived up there with bears for four months at a time, twenty-four hours a day for thirteen years without a scratch. I think he finally just met the wrong bear."

There was a long pause before Roland continued, "There are just a lot of things about Timothy that people don't know. Things that even I didn't know until lately. And they've got to come out. The public thinks he's just another nut and a crackpot, and he's not. He's done an incredible job of teaching the public about bears, especially the kids. I had him come up to Colorado, and we'd do five grade schools each day, five days per week. And we'd do it for months at a time. Tim didn't do so well with teenagers, though. He liked to be in control, and he couldn't [be] with the bigger kids. He did a little better with grown-ups, but they made him awful nervous and jumpy, but the grade school kids absolutely loved him. They'd flock around him like the Pied Piper. He's taught thousands of schoolkids the true nature of the grizzly. People who badmouth him don't know that he accomplished this to . . . to the detriment of his health."

"What do you mean?" I asked.

"Well . . . ," Roland struggled to find the right words. "Timmy had emotional problems. He'd be on top of the world, then way down in the dumps. I've seen him so depressed that I really worried about his well-being. Then he'd work his way out of it. He's told me things that have been complete fabrications. I think they were an outcome of his depression. When he was depressed he was really a lot more emotional than when he was feeling on top of things. I had several talks with him about it, but it didn't help.

"There's been a lot of bad press about him doing outlandish things around bears from the films he released to the public, but Grizzly People [the grassroots grizzly conservation organization created by Timothy and Jewel Palovak, coauthor of his book] has got a lot of film that the public has never seen. A lot of it shows Timmy doing some really wild things when he was not in control and very emotional. It was really scary. I finally sat him down and told him that if he didn't seek professional help, I'd cut off his funding. Tim promised to get help, but he never did.

"Don't get me wrong. Tim wasn't crazy. In fact, just the opposite; he was very lucid, but he wasn't always in control of his emotions, and if you saw some of the films I saw, you'd agree."

I told Roland that I'd followed Timothy's career and had feared for Timothy's safety just from the scenes I saw on television. Roland replied, "That's nothing compared to the stuff that's been kept out of the public eye. I'm on the board of directors of Grizzly People, and we just had a big phone conference. I told them that we had to come out with the films and show them to the public. It's the only way to show how much Timmy really loved the bears, and how impassioned he was, and how hard he tried to do what was right. People say he was crazy, but he wasn't. He just had a neurological disorder. A lot of time he wasn't in control.

"I really believe that the deprivation that Timmy endured for four months at a time—the cold and the rain, eating peanut butter and jelly sandwiches for months at a time—it was his way of dealing with his mental condition. However bad it was up there, it eased the pain that was deep inside him. I remember looking at a film segment where Tim was edging close to a sow grizzly feeding her cubs, and it looked like Tim's face was blurry, as if the camera was out of focus. Then I saw this huge cloud of mosquitoes that was engulfing his face. How could a guy put up with that for months on end unless the alternative was even worse?

"I've also learned another side of Timmy since his death. He fabricated a lot of stuff. He told varying stories about his life. He told me that he had a secret agreement with Katmai officials that if he was killed by a bear, the officials wouldn't kill the bear."

Roland Dixon's voice is suddenly hard. "And he lied to me about Amie. I told him under no circumstances could she accompany him. He said she wouldn't, but he took her up there anyway. I love the guy and believe in his vision, but right now I'm very angry with him. It was absolutely immoral of him to have sent her up there with no protection because there's no way she could have known what she was getting herself into. If I was her family, I'd be furious about her death. It was so needless. I was always after him to carry bear spray and string an electrical fence around his camp. He said he would, but he never did. Hell, even Charlie Russell uses an electric fence around his place in Russia."

I asked Roland why he was telling me all this. "I don't know. For some reason I trust you to tell the truth about Timmy and not sensationalize everything. I really love the guy and it's frustrating to hear all the bad things about him. He was not a bad person. In fact, he was wonderful. That's why I want the other films released to the public. I want to show the world that Timmy had an emotional problem, but he loved the bears, and we shouldn't let his vision of protecting the bears die with him. It would have crushed him to know that he was responsible for two bears dying."

Our phone conversation ended cordially, and I promised to send Roland a book I wrote about elk behavior. Afterwards, I sat stunned, my mind racing over the implications and ramifications of our conversation. If Roland Dixon was right, Timothy Treadwell's preoccupation with getting close to bears was not the arrogant act of a self-centered glory hound, as most of his detractors claimed. Instead, it was the only way a troubled man could ease his pain while striving to do something good in his life.

I was also struck by the bravery of the man who filled me in on the Timothy Treadwell no one knew. Surely, Roland Dixon would take heat from the pro-Treadwell camp. But I truly believe his intentions were noble: that he was willing to give up his life, so to speak, for a friend—which in this case meant his good standing among his peers so that he might show the world the emotional struggle that Timothy Treadwell endured in his private life.

Others who encountered Timothy also noticed the darker side of Timothy's spirit, though they struggled to explain it—this "something" that seemed to haunt his consuming desire to get close to the bears. Wanetta Ayers, who initially considered Timothy to be "kind of goofy" when he approached her at the Kodiak Visitors Center, would later become his advocate and protector. "I've tried to understand what made Timothy so different," she wrote in a letter to the *Anchorage Press* shortly after his death. "When he rediscovered himself in the Alaska wilderness, under the good graces of the bears that surrounded him for so long, he undoubtedly tested and faced his greatest fear, which was not of living with the grizzlies, but of living with himself."

My review of Timothy's films and writings, and interviews with some of those closest to him, coupled with my own experiences in the mental health field as a lay counselor, have led me to some of my own conclusions about the demons that reportedly dogged Treadwell. Bipolar disorder seems to match the long record of behaviors Timothy exhibited. People with bipolar disorder are often difficult to identify because they act quite normal, other than they tend to be overly effusive, charming, and self-confident, then moody—symptoms not unusual among humans. The difference is that a person with bipolar disorder experiences cycles of manic then depressive activity, regardless of circumstances. Bipolar disorder is simply a neurological imbalance in the brain that produces an excess of chemicals, which result in a state of near euphoria followed by a slow, eroding process that eventually blocks those chemicals, and the person is so depressed that he feels trapped in the bottom of a dark emotional pit. Then it's back up, then back down.

The Depression Sourcebook notes several bipolar symptoms that would specifically pertain to Timothy Treadwell. At times he had an inflated sense of self-esteem and overconfidence. He was charismatic, persuasive, and witty. His moods were often infectious and drew people to him. He felt an exquisite sense of communion with nature. He was considered a workaholic (such as when traveling from school to school to educate children about bears). He was taking risks that the average mentally healthy person would not take. He found himself minimizing the risks of his behavior and rationalizing his actions. He insisted everyone was worrying too much. He criticized the people who cautioned him as being uptight and jealous.

This subject also hits close to home. A dear friend of mine has a mild form of bipolar disorder—one that affects thousands of Americans and is easily treatable with medication and therapy.

I asked my friend to read Timothy Treadwell's book and study the documentary footage. He commented, "It's obvious to me he was suffering from some kind of bipolar disorder. In his book he writes about lying around with bears right next to him while he sings love songs to them, then he's weeping and hating himself for being such a miserable human being. Up and down, up and down. When I watched all that footage of him close to those bears, I was thinking, 'It doesn't matter whether he's manic or depressive. If he's up, he thinks he's invincible and the bears can't hurt him, and if he's down, he really doesn't give a damn whether he lives or dies.' I'll bet those bears could sense that in him, that he either didn't think they could kill him, or didn't care."

My friend continued, "Another thing about bipolar [disorder] is that people who have it are often so miserable that they gravitate to the unfortunate and disadvantaged. With Timothy Treadwell it was, 'Poor Grizzly! I'll protect you. I can't do anything to save my plight in life, but at least I can save you.'

"Adrenaline's the big thing that I think made Timothy Treadwell move so close to the bears. When I was in high school, I was always in sports because it was non-stop adrenaline. It was the one [thing] that helped me when I was on the down side. It made it easier for me to forget about it. Sometimes when we had a big game, I'd be on the low side and the adrenaline high of the game took me right through my low time to the point where I totally missed the depression.

"I don't agree with what Timothy did, but I have an empathy for him. He wasn't having a lot of fun out there. He was enduring it because the alternative was worse. In a way those bears did save his life, like he claimed, but not because they got him off alcohol. He'd have somehow killed himself without the self-medication those adrenaline rushes gave him. At least now he's at peace."

I shared with my friend some of the details Carol Dexter confided about Timothy's childhood. Those details added up to a clearer picture for my friend. He commented, "Even his younger years showed signs. He was hyper, he loved fireworks and fighting [typical early signs of bipolar disorder], and he got lost in fantasies. I was the same way as a kid. I was always being kept in during recess and lunch hour because of some euphoric outburst during class. While the other kids were outside playing, I got lost in my own fantasy world of army tanks and bombs and flying jet airplanes at war."

To get a professional opinion on this matter, I met with psychologist and outdoorsman Jim Ramsey—himself a resident of western Montana and therefore no stranger to black and grizzly bears. I filled him in about Timothy's hyperactive personality, his early years of frustration with being dyslexic, his tendency toward symptoms of ADD, his binge drinking and drug addiction, and finally his fits of depression and elation. Ramsey offered his opinion.

"From [what you've told me], I'd say he was probably bipolar. And bipolar people are often addicted to drugs. They use them to get through the depressive stage. He had an addictive personality. He was addicted to action, addicted to alcohol, addicted to drugs. And the first time he came face to face with a grizzly, he became addicted to the adrenaline rush of the close encounter. People don't understand how powerful adrenaline is to the human body. In men it's as strong as the sex urge. That's why men sit in front of the television watching sports— for the adrenaline rush of seeing someone score a touchdown or hit a home run. With Timothy adrenaline salved over his depression.

"Once he experienced that first adrenaline-gushing close bear encounter, he was hooked. And there was no way that he was going to sit back and methodically study bears. He wanted to be RIGHT THERE, because he's not going to get an adrenaline rush if he's 300 yards away.

"Since he was never tested by a psychiatrist, we can only conjecture, but his friend's [Roland Dixon's] testimony is a strong indication that he had something. It's hard to say whether he had extreme or mild bipolar disorder, or how often he was manic-depressive. The one thing we do know is that, left untreated, bipolar disorder only gets worse. It's hard to say what stage it was at when he died. And it doesn't surprise me that Timothy Treadwell refused to get help. That's common among people with bipolar disorder because they don't want to lose the exquisite high when they're manic."

I didn't call Carol Dexter back to discuss any of these conclusions with her. I left her instead with good memories of her son, the kind a mother should have. I wanted her to remember the positive highlights of her son's life, such as the one reflected in her first phone conversation with Timothy after he returned from his initial trip to Alaska. "He was so excited!" she declared. "He told me, 'I found my god, mom. I finally found something to live for.' He was just absolutely in love with Alaska and the wilderness. He told me he finally found something to take the place of alcohol in his life, and he quit drinking. I was really glad to hear that."

Carol also remembers the day in October 2003 when she returned to her Pompano Beach, Florida, home to find a police cruiser parked across the street. "I figured there was a problem at the neighbors, but when I walked into the house, there was a man and a lady officer there. My ninety-seven-year-old father and [my husband] Val were sitting at the table—and the look on their faces told me something was wrong. They made me sit down before they broke the news that Timmy had been killed by a bear. I was absolutely devastated. The whole family was in shock. It took a long time for my husband and I to accept the fact that Timmy was gone."

Carol sighs loudly and adds, "We've kept a low profile and stayed out of all the controversy. It hurts too much. I prefer to think the best of my boy. And when I miss him I go out the back door to a canal that runs past our house. I have ducks there that I feed. They love me, and I love them. That's where Timmy got his love for animals. He got it from me. Some of the ducks let me hold them and kiss them. One duck is my favorite. I named him Timmy."

CHAPTER 9

Tragedy Stalks the Grizzly Maze

IN ONE WAY TIMOTHY TREADWELL was right about bears. They're very much like humans. When times are good both species tend to be relatively benign, their mannerisms laid back, even serene. But threaten their way of life, and both species can be dangerous. There are desperate human beings, just as there are desperate bears.

For a bear the basic instinct to survive is all-powerful. A bear's well-being depends upon its next meal. A bear's world is so defined by food that to forgo one meal sends an instinctive shudder through its system. Every meal that is missed means fat that won't be available during hibernation when bitter cold and deep snow bury the land. It often doesn't take much to see a bear's worst side. Just take away its food.

By late August 2003 Timothy Treadwell was beginning to see that side of the bears at Kaflia Bay, or, as he called it, the Grizzly Maze. The bears that had lazed side by side through the enormous salmon spawning runs were growing testy with each other as the food supply dwindled.

Timothy had been there for a month, during which he'd reveled in the sight of dozens of bears gorging on salmon while ignoring each other, and Treadwell himself. But as the salmon runs dwindled through August, bears that had seemingly welcomed each other's company now turned on each other. Timothy noted in his diary that a female bear desperate to feed her hungry cubs made the mistake of fishing too close to a dominant male. The big male attacked, tearing at her with powerful jaws and pounding her with sledgehammer blows. Barely half the big male's size, the female bear initially went down under the male bear's ferocious attack, but she fought back until the big male stepped back, lest he receive a wound that might threaten his survival. The battered female loped off with her cubs.

On August 21 Timothy penned a frantic note in his journal, revealing his trepidation: "Much danger for me. I feel a great deal of paranoia, and rightfully so. Some 500 yards away, the creek is loaded with bears and trouble. The chemistry between the bears is explosive—three killer bears . . . I feel the tension growing."

Timothy's assessment proved accurate. With only a few salmon splashing up the main creek the next morning, a tremendous fight broke out among dominant bears and spread to subdominant males as the beaten bigger males took out their frustrations on lesser bears that in turn bullied smaller females, cubs, and subadults. It was not a safe place for a young bear, especially a cub. Consequently, the female bears kept to the alders and emerged only after first studying the surrounding terrain for bigger bears.

The brutal battles between competing males seemed to have heightened Timothy's excitement, and on August 25 he sent out a note to Roland Dixon: "I am in the most exciting and dangerous time of my . . . fieldwork. I am so deep within the brown bear culture. It is fascinating, beautiful, and at times treacherous."

Timothy was seeing the grizzlies as he'd never before seen them—hungry, desperate, deadly. The most aggressive bears dominated the other bears that were not fighters. Some bears, like humans, tend to be passive, and violence scares them. The female bear that Timothy had named Downey was one such bear. Unwilling or unable to defend herself, she sought refuge in those out-of-the-way areas rarely visited by the more dominant bears because there was less food there. Carrying his video equipment with him, Timothy went searching one day in late August for Downey, who had disappeared from the area near the creek. Timothy found her foraging along a small stream, frightened by every rustling in the brush, spooked by every sudden noise. That Downey would allow him to move in close to her was not extraordinary. She knew from past encounters that he was harmless.

With the camera running and Downey first nosing at it then wandering into the background, Timothy stepped in front of the lens and said, "Downey is seven years old, and I've known her since she was a spring pup, like she was my own sister." Timothy studied the bear for a while and said, "You are the most beautiful thing." Then he turned back to the camera and spoke in a strained voice, "And I will care for her. I will live for her. I will die for her." Tears welled and spilled down his cheeks.

In Timothy's view, it wasn't supposed to be like this: bears biting and tearing at each other, trying to kill each other. They—the bears and man—were all supposed be family, living together, feeding together, sleeping together. What about all the years they'd spent getting to know each other? Had it all been in vain? Where was the love?

Love was due to arrive the next day when a Sea Otter floatplane dropped off Amie Huguenard. On this night, however, Timothy wrote Roland Dixon a letter—his last—not mentioning that Amie Huguenard was on her way to Alaska. The letter proved to be a stunning, troubling—and prophetic—document:

Roland,

Hello! I am writing you a last letter for the journey. My last food delivery is scheduled for late today.

My transformation is complete—a fully accepted wild animal-brother to these bears. I run free among them—with absolute love and respect for all animals. I am kind and viciously tough.

People—especially the bear experts of Alaska—believe this cannot be done. Some even bet on my death. They are sure you must have some sort of weapon for defense—pepper spray at the least, an electric fence a must. And you cannot hope to make it in a flimsy tent under thick cover among one of the earth's largest gatherings of giant brown grizzly bears.

People who knowingly enter bear habitat with pepper spray, guns, and electric fences are committing a crime to the animals. They begin with the accepted idea of bringing instruments of pain to the animals. If they are that fearful, then they have no place in the land of this perfect animal.

How could I look at Dixon [a bear Treadwell named for Roland], Lilly, and her mother, Melissa, and tell that I love them, that I care for them, with a can of mace in my back pocket?

The morning after Timothy Treadwell tucked this note into an envelope, the beginning of his end began to unravel from the whole cloth that may have been the fabric of his life. No one knows for sure exactly what happened next, but it is known that Amie Huguenard arrived at ten o'clock the next morning, on September 14, 2003. Timothy handed pilot Willy Fulton the letter addressed to Roland Dixon.

The entire world that Timothy called the Grizzly Maze was upside down when Amie arrived. After a furious fight the big male Timothy called Demon had supplanted another dominant male that Timothy had named the Big Red Machine because of its reddish, matted fur. While the Machine seethed in exile, Demon patrolled the main creek that still held a few salmon, foaming at the mouth and rushing any bear that dared approach.

Instead of heading for the main creek where most of the bears had hung out in the past, Timothy steered Amie off to the east toward the secluded creeks and side bays where Downey and some of the sows with cubs, and subadults, had taken refuge, but Downey was missing. Over the next few days, Timothy's mood darkened further when he still couldn't find the bear. Had she just moved off to another isolated cove, or had one of the big males pounced on her? But then his mood brightened, and he became effusive as he filmed himself approaching within arm's length of those few bears that had allowed him that liberty. He even urged Amie to move close to a few of them, though she loathed being on camera. One time during this period in mid-September, while Amie was out near the shoreline watching some bears, she turned around and found that Tim was not at her side but was filming her from a distance; her expression said, "Everything's okay, isn't it?"

Amie had other animal problems besides bears. She detested the weasels that besieged their tent as soon as the lantern was turned off. Resembling a sort of furry dachshund with sharp teeth, the tiny varmints were just beginning to turn into ermine, trading their summer brown fur for a brilliant white pelage that would camouflage them from predator and prey through the snowy winter. The smallest opening was enough for an ermine to gain access to the tent, and if there were no holes, the ermine's needle-sharp teeth made one. Timothy wrote in his diary, "These wormy animals are kicking my ass. More than once I've jumped up in the middle of the night and chased them into the bushes with a stick."

The changing of the season brought unsettled weather to Kaflia Bay. Cold, torrential rains pounded the Grizzly Maze, and at times the inhabitants of the tent couldn't tell whether it was the blustery wind rattling the alders outside the tent or a passing grizzly. The rain brought even more weasels seeking the warm dryness of the tent. It also brought an onslaught of other critters that Amie detested— spiders. She couldn't get rid of them fast enough—wolf spiders, crab spiders, orb spiders—all innocuous, but for a spider hater it was hell.

The fall rains had also resulted in an explosion of mosquitoes, and clouds of the bloodthirsty airborne vampires descended upon Timothy and Amie whenever it stopped raining. Tim had become oblivious to their insidious buzzing, biting presence. Amie, on the other hand, loathed the mosquitoes, but she endured their maddening assaults stoically, though often with a mosquito net over her head and gloves on her hands.

Despite Amie's protests Timothy continued pursuing the largest brown bears with his camera. In one bit of footage, Timothy eased forward, stopping when the big bear raised his huge, shaggy head and cast a baleful glare his way. When Demon went back to swatting at a passing salmon, Timothy slipped forward and set up the camera 50 yards from the bear. Demon got lucky and crippled a salmon. With a sudden lunge the bear snatched the salmon from the water and began tearing it apart on the shore. With the bear preoccupied Timothy eased forward and into the picture. He spoke in a hushed voice, "It is said that giant male bears do not allow any animal near their food source. I am being let in very close to Demon and his food source. And, in a further sign that he trusts me, he has actually turned his back on me."

By the time Timothy stopped filming this event, the big bear was almost done eating the fish. Amie was beside herself with anxiety, frantically gesturing to him to get out of there. Timothy was still jumpy with nervous excitement and decided that they should continue searching for Downey. They spent the rest of the day in a fruitless search. The next day it rained, and Timothy's mood darkened with every hour that they searched. Downey was nowhere to be found.

Timothy had made arrangements in advance for them to be flown out the next morning, but Downey's absence put a pall on the tent that night. The next morning, Willy Fulton picked them up and took them to Kodiak by floatplane. The plan was for Amie and Timothy to fly to Anchorage and then rent a car and tour Denali National Park, photographing the late fall scenery and bears as they went. Timothy was still glum when they approached the ticket counter. Dark, brooding clouds were rolling in. Dark clouds meant rain, and rain meant fuller creeks, and fuller creeks meant more salmon for all the bears, and maybe even for Downey. He strode to a pay phone and called Jewel Palovak and told her that he was staying to find Downey. Amie would stay, too.

The storm brought pounding rain and high winds, grounding all small aircraft. Amie and Timothy waited out the storm in Kodiak for three days, but at the first sign of a letup, they hurried over to Andrew Airways. On the morning of September 29, 2003, owner Dean Andrew found Amie and Timothy waiting in his aircraft hangar when he arrived. As long as Treadwell paid, he was more than happy to fly the eccentric bear lover around. But that morning he was curious about why the two of them were heading back to the same place they'd just left, and so late in the year. "Tim just told me they hadn't said their proper good-byes," Andrews recalls. "Still, I thought it was a little odd because he normally stuck to a pretty rigid schedule."

When they arrived back at the Grizzly Maze, things had gone from bad to worse. There were no bears along the beach. When Amie and Timothy waded ashore, they discovered why. Almost no salmon were in the main creek. Most of the bears had moved inland, picking at rancid salmon skeletons and scouring the berry bushes for non-existent fruit while they slowly migrated toward the high mountain slopes to hibernate.

Bears were crunching through the brush all around the small opening where Timothy insisted they set up their small blue sleeping tent, with another small tent a few feet away where they stored their food and supplies and ate their meals. Bears had filtered through the area in the past, but not like this. There seemed to always be a bear within earshot—snapping brush, huffing, growling. Even though the campsite was at the crossroads of several main bear trails, Timothy insisted that they camp there because the alder brush provided some relief from the winds. Amie hadn't liked the site the last time because any passing bear had to walk right by their tent, and a few times they were awakened in the middle of the night by the huffing of a passing bear. But now, it was worse. Bears huffed and crunched brush nearby even while they set up their camp.

One factor that had taken a turn for the better was Timothy's mood. He was once again expressive and talkative, telling Amie that this would be their best bear trip yet. Amie was happy, too, sure that his sudden mood change came from the prospect of finding the missing Downey bear. That was all well and good, but she still didn't like the way the bears were acting.

As they wandered along a series of small inlets that morning, Timothy urged Amie to hunker down behind a large alder bush 10 yards from shore as a bear with two cubs worked their way toward her. Timothy hurried back about 40 yards and set up the camera. Amie did well until the bears were almost even with her, then at the last second she leaned away, in obvious discomfort with having the bears so close.

That afternoon, Timothy tried again to urge Amie to hunker down behind a large driftwood jumble as a subadult bear worked his way along a small creek, but Amie refused. Timothy didn't lose his expansive mood.

The fourth of October dawned clear and cold. The temperature was thirty-eight degrees, not far from frosting. Before long, snow would cover the land, and the bears knew it. They were obsessed with food. A few found salmon, but others now crunched fish skeletons, rotting seaweed, clam shells—anything that might have food value. The sun finally burst over the mountain, bathing Kaflia Bay in warm autumn sunlight.

On their morning search for Downey, a short distance below camp, they pushed through the alders to a small creek and spotted a subadult male about 60 yards away on the opposite side of the stream. They had to pass by the bear to check one of the back bays where Downey often hung out. But as they eased forward, the young bear turned toward them—his head down, shoulders squared—in an aggressive posture.

As they moved around the aggressive bear, 100 yards away stood the bear named Downey, swiping at a few salmon that had become trapped in a small pool at the mouth of a side stream. Timothy set up the camera and recorded Downey catching a salmon and hungrily devouring it. Timothy exulted in Downey's presence, filming her and singing love songs as the bear cocked her head in puzzlement. So excited was Timothy that he paid no attention when a tremendous bear fight erupted back at the main creek. The bear called Demon stood stiffly, hair raising along his neck and shoulders. A deep, guttural sound rumbled from his throat as he watched the bear called the Big Red Machine slowly advance on the opposite shore. Belly empty and growling, the Machine was inexorably drawn to the splashing of salmon and the tantalizing emergence of a tail above the surface.

The bears stood just a few feet apart, their ears laid back, hair on end, warning growls and throaty huffs emanating from both of them. Demon advanced slowly, but the red bear refused to back up. The splash of a salmon at his feet distracted the red bear, and he glanced down. In that instant the Demon bear attacked, swatting the red bear's face and knocking him backward. The Demon bear lunged with teeth snapping, but the red bear landed a savage blow to the left side of his adversary's head. Demon bellowed in rage and pain and sprang at the red bear, coming in low, his massive jaws snapping at the red bear's soft underbelly. The red bear bellowed in pain as the Demon bear bit into the soft hide just below the rib cage. The red bear jumped up, biting and swatting as he retreated. Then he whirled and dove into the alders with the Demon bear in close pursuit.

In the afternoon, storm clouds rolled in and the rain came down, so Amie and Timothy retired to their tent. Timothy phoned Andrew Airways by satellite phone, asking for Willy Fulton to come and get them because Willy knew exactly where they were. The next morning, Sunday, October 5, Timothy phoned Jewel Palovak and had her call Alaska Airlines. She reserved two adjoining seats for October 7 for Amie and Timothy out of Kodiak. The flight destination was Los Angeles, where Amie would be starting her new job in a week—a half-hour drive from the new apartment she and Timothy would be sharing.

They left the tent and braved the rain for only a short time, checking for Downey at the side bay. She wasn't there but the subadult bear that had false-charged them the day before was there. He studied them intensely, so they backed off and headed for the main creek. Demon was still there, guarding the mouth of the creek, but he seemed bothered and several times pawed at his left ear. When Timothy looked through his binoculars, he could see blood, and it appeared that half the ear was gone. Back at the tent, they shucked their wet clothes and hung them in the supply tent to dry. An occasional bear woofed and huffed nearby. This is what I think happened next.

The big red bear pushed through a tunnel and stopped in a narrow opening overlooking the main creek below. The Demon bear was still down there, pacing back and forth and rubbing at his ear. The red bear swung his shaggy head and spotted the subadult male pawing at a salmon skeleton along the shore of the side bay. The red bear studied the terrain down to the side bay. A sizable trail wound down through the alders, and the bear eased his half-ton bulk downhill, moving slowly to avoid kicking loose a rock.

The subadult bear heard a noise behind him and spotted the smallish female that he'd chased away earlier in the day. Popping his teeth, he advanced toward her with head low and beady eyes locked on her. The female backed away, then galloped off through the brush. The young bear turned back and coughed several times to clear fish bones from his throat. He spotted the rotting head of a salmon wedged down between two hundred-pound rocks. With a mighty tug he rolled one of the boulders back.

As the young bear dropped his head and opened his mouth to snatch the rancid fish head, a tremendous blow sent him flying. The young bear bawled in anger and fear and spun around just in time to catch another glancing blow from the big red bear. Still, the blow knocked the young bear onto his side. The red bear pounced on his prey, mouth agape as he lunged for the young bear's throat, but the loose boulder rolled back into place, knocking the red bear sideways, and his teeth snapped shut on the young bear's left shoulder. Bellowing in pain, the young bear regained his feet and scrambled over the loose rocks. The big red bear tried to gallop after him, but his weight sent some of the loose rocks clattering under his feet, allowing the young bear to dive into the safety of the alders.

The big red bear spun and swatted the boulder, sending it spinning for several feet. Then the bear sniffed the air, and saliva drooled from his open mouth. He put his nose to the rocks and sniffed deeply at the sticky red smear. He licked the blood off the rock, then followed the scent to the next blood smear and did the same.

The young bear stopped and raised his head, listening. Nothing. Then he heard it, the soft shuffling sound that had been coming from his back trail for the past half-hour. A branch snapped, brush swished, and the young bear bolted ahead through the brush. He ran for a hundred yards and stopped at the edge of a small opening. He was tired and his shoulder ached. He licked the seep of blood from the gash that the big, red bear had inflicted. A branch snapped behind him and he jumped. The big red bear was back there, still following him.

The young bear stepped into the opening to put more distance between himself and the big red bear and let out a "Huff!" when he saw the blue tent just 20 feet away.

There were voices inside the tent, and the brush behind him began to snap and crackle again. The big red bear that had pounced on him minutes earlier was back there—following him. The young bear bounced forward, pounding his paws on the ground and huffing.

There was loud yelling from the tent now, and the young bear jumped back and started to turn away. But the sound of the big red bear's labored breathing as it trudged up the hill sent him back the other way. A half-bawl, half-frightened roar blasted from the frantic bear's throat.

Timothy zipped open the tent door and gingerly stepped outside onto the cold, wet grass. At first, he saw nothing. He'd thought the bear was directly in front of the door. Then he smelled it—rotting fish. He turned to his right and spotted the young bear 15 feet way. It was just a small bear, though it had a frightened, hunted look in its eyes.

Timothy yelled, rising to his full height, spreading his arms to look bigger. He took a few quick steps toward the bear and yelled more.

The young bear lunged, and the man spun away. But the blow caught him on the left shoulder, sending him sprawling. And then the young bear was on him, ripping and tearing with its jaws; the threats from the man and the big red bear had stressed him to the limit.

Amie's voice came from the tent. The only reply was a strangled grunt amidst the violent swishing of alders and the thud of heavy bodies pounding the ground. Then there was shrieking and the loud cries of Timothy asking for help.

Timothy's voice ripped through the air. "Come out here!" Then a loud shriek and another cry, "I'm being killed out here!"

A small animal cry escaped from Amie's throat as she fumbled with the door zipper. She gasped when she saw Timothy lying on his back, a smallish bear biting at his arms and hands as he fought it.

"Play dead!" Amie screeched. When she saw the blood all over his head and arms, she began to wail, and the bear jumped back. But when Timothy began to rise, the bear pounced on him again, tearing at his shoulder and shaking him violently.

Screaming and crying, Amie yelled, "Fight back!"

Timothy lay gasping as the bear continued ravaging him. "Hit . . . hit it with a frying pan," came his tortured reply.

Shock sent her stumbling back against the tent, screaming and wailing hysterically as she watched the horrid scene before her. Instinctively, she grabbed a walking stick and rapped the bear on the back. The last thing she saw was the bear turning and swinging . . . The final six minutes of their lives were recorded in horrid detail by the camera's audio, though the lens cap was still in place.

The big red bear smelled the blood before he reached the opening. The young bear heard the oncoming brute and scampered away. The red bear dragged Timothy's body back down the trail and fed on it, then came back and cached the other body—using a covering of sticks and leaves and dirt to conceal it from scavenging birds and other predators.

When the big red bear left the cache and went down to the creek for a drink, the young bear hurried forward and gorged itself until it heard the big red bear returning.

Calm returned to the Grizzly Maze later that night. The big red bear curled up atop its cache, and the young bear snoozed in a thicket a short distance away.

CHAPTER 10

Guns Trump Love
at Kaflia Bay

As an Alaskan bush pilot, Willy Fulton lives on the edge—of glaciers, of blizzards, of a land so breathtakingly beautiful that it's easy to forget that at any moment your life can be on the line. A powerful thermal downdraft might threaten to suck your plane into the jagged rocks below. But more often the danger begins with subtle clues—as if the land is testing your mettle. Is the oil gauge merely sticking, or is that precious black lubricant spewing out of the engine into the cold sea air? Are your ears just popping from the high altitude, or is the popping sound a crack in the wing?

Willy Fulton has survived a long time in Alaska's most dangerous profession by quickly analyzing and reacting to the slightest nuance. As the Beaver floatplane flew in and out of dense cloud banks hovering low over the Katmai Coast on the afternoon of Monday, October 6, 2003, he was flying with the knowledge that Timothy Treadwell had not called in that morning, a fact just enough out of the ordinary to make him take notice.

Timothy was more than a client to Willy. During the years he'd spent flying Timothy around Katmai, the two men had become friends. The same with Amie Huguenard, even though she was a relative newcomer to Katmai. They sometimes stayed at Willy's place whenever they were coming or going to Katmai.

Timothy always called before a pick up to let Willy know what the wind and weather was like at the pick-up site. Maybe the batteries had gone out on Tim's satellite phone that morning, or maybe he simply forgot to call to confirm their plans.

As the Beaver banked sharply and swooped down into the narrow inlet where he'd dropped off Amie and Timothy a few days earlier, Willy saw an empty beach. Tim always had his gear meticulously stacked and waiting at the prearranged pick-up site, so as not to hold up Willy a moment longer than necessary.

Up on the hill, the big red bear studied the floatplane bobbing against the logjam. A gust of wind rattled the alders, which unleashed a fresh surge of icy cold water splashing against the animal's face. The bear shook the moisture from his eyes and peered down through the alders that had overnight lost most of their leaves. A deep warning rumbled from the big red bear's chest as he watched the man below wade ashore and start up the hill.

Willy Fulton could see movement up at the campsite. It looked like Timothy was shaking out a tarp. He brought a hand up to shield his eyes and squinted to better see the movement up on the hill. It wasn't a man moving up on the hill at the Treadwell campsite. It was a bear.

Maybe a bear had taken over Treadwell's camp during the night and Tim and Amie had slipped away. They'd stumble out of the brush at any moment, tired and wet, but as alive and sassy as ever. But happy endings were rare out here in the Alaskan bush when things went wrong.

Willy pushed up through the alders looking for Tim and Amie. He'd gone only about 50 yards when he heard the brush snapping, distant at first, but growing increasingly loud and violent by the second. Willy charged back downhill. The terrifying explosion of breaking brush was almost upon him when he stumbled onto the beach and sprinted for the Beaver.

"Huff! Huff! Huff!" The guttural sounds were right behind him, but he didn't bother to look back. He knew what was behind him. He splashed into the water and hopped onto one of the Beaver's floats. When he looked back a big reddish bear had skidded to a halt less than 10 feet away, popping its massive jaws and growling.

Willy opened the door and climbed into the cockpit. He started the Beaver's engine, and the bear backed away, but not far. The engine revved loudly. The big red bear backed away and moved into the brush.

Willy put the Beaver into the air and circled over the camp. Both tents were flattened, and a few bear-proof containers lay strewn around. A huge mound of fresh dirt had been piled just a few feet from the blue tent, and the big red bear was standing on it. Willy buzzed the campsite about twenty times, hoping to drive the bear away, but the animal refused to leave. Instead it hunched down and pawed at the dirt.

Ninety miles away, ranger Joel Ellis was at his desk at park head-quarters in King Salmon when he took the phone call that park offi-cials feared would someday come. It was the dispatcher at Andrew Airways out at the airport in Kodiak. He'd just received a call from one of their pilots, Willy Fulton, who said he couldn't find two of his clients for a pick up, and that there was a big bear at the abandoned campsite, and that it looked like the bear might be feeding on human remains, and that one of the missing people was Timothy Treadwell.

Ellis kept his outward calm and asked the caller to have Willy stay where he was if he could do so safely. He hung up the phone and had park dispatch relay the report to the state troopers at King Salmon and to the Alaska Fish and Game Department. He then phoned park pilot Allen Gilliland to prepare for a flight to the coast and hurried to find ranger Derek Dalrymple, but he wasn't in his office. The dispatcher finally located Dalrymple and told him they'd received a report of a missing camper. Dalrymple was to hurry to the office, and he should bring his shotgun.

The Park Service's Cessna 206 floatplane with the three men aboard left its mooring and roared off the choppy, windswept waters into a low cloud bank and pelting rain. Joel Ellis checked his watch. It was 3:20 P.M.—late in the day for a search party in the north country where twilight gathers early, but they had no choice.

An hour later the Cessna banked hard and dropped into the narrow mountainous bowl that forms Kaflia Bay. Willy Fulton's orange Beaver floatplane was bobbing offshore. Fulton told the rangers that he was actually a mile west of Treadwell's campsite. "I flew over the campsite after the bear chased me off," Willy informed the rangers, "and that big red bear had a cache scraped up right next to Tim's blue sleeping tent. I couldn't be a hundred percent sure, but it looked like the bear was feeding on a body."

Fulton told pilot Gilliland that the landing site was too narrow for both planes, so Joel Ellis told Willy to hop in with them. Ten minutes later the Cessna taxied to the south shore below Treadwell's campsite. The men, wearing hip boots and raincoats, waded ashore. Gilliland and Dalrymple carried twelve-gauge pump shotguns loaded with rifled slugs. Such a firearm was woefully inadequate at a range beyond 50 yards, but for quick close-range shooting at dangerous game, the massive one-ounce slug could blast a fist-sized hole into any charging bear.

The big red bear lay on the mound of freshly churned earth and eyed the men below. His belly was full to bulging, the first time it had felt so full since he'd lost his feeding place to the other big bear down at the mouth of the salmon stream. As the men started moving in his direction, the big red bear's head jerked up, and a low rumbling began in his throat. The meat hidden under the dirt would sustain him until the snows came, and he would fight to the death to keep it for himself. He rose, paws sinking into the soft black dirt.

Brush began snapping and crackling below him. Human voices—loud and tense—raised the hair on his neck. "Huff! Huff!" he warned them to stay away, but the swish of brush came closer, until he could stand it no longer. With a loud grunt he hurtled into the dense alder tangle below.

Allen Gilliland heard the bear coming through the alders before he saw it. Suddenly, an enormous red bear appeared just 20 yards away, and Gilliland yelled, "Bear!" All four men started yelling, hoping to turn the animal back the way it had come, but their frantic yelling seemed only to enrage the big red bear more, and he came harder. Gilliland snapped the shotgun to his shoulder. Dalrymple did the same. Joel Ellis saw the men with their rifles up and pointed his pistol at the bear, who had zeroed in on Gilliland and was picking up speed. The guns fired almost as one. The volley staggered the bear but did not stop it. Another volley smashed into it, and the bear fell, then rose in time to catch two more slugs in its chest and a pistol slug in its paunch. Twice more the rangers fired, until the bear slumped to the ground just four paces from Joel Ellis's feet. After a few shudders the bear lay still.

Another floatplane landed, and state troopers Hill and Jones waded ashore and began moving uphill. The three park rangers and Fulton pushed their way up to the campsite. Both tents had been flattened by bears, and the mounded food cache was just a few feet in front of the blue tent's door. Four bear-proof containers lay scattered around the campsite, but they had not been opened by the bears.

Gilliland climbed onto the bear's cache and took several deep breaths, then he began to dig into the soft dirt with a stick. Remains of a human arm appeared, and the men grew silent, finally acknowledging what they had been hoping and praying against. Water was trapped in large pools on top of the tents, so Ellis sliced open the sides with his knife and peeked inside, hoping to find a human. He found only camping gear and sleeping bags.

Ellis and Dalrymple returned to the park plane to get cameras to record the scene of the tragedy. The men had no sooner left when a large brown bear emerged from a clump of willows above the camp and began moving steadily toward Gilliland and Fulton. Rangers Ellis and Dalrymple watched helplessly from the Cessna's floats as the drama unfolded on the hill above them.

Gilliland snapped the shotgun to his shoulder and flipped off the safety. The bear continued toward them—30 yards, then 20, then 10. But the bear's body language was more relaxed and showed no sign of aggression, so Gilliland held back from squeezing the trigger. The bear continued ambling along and passed just 15 feet away, casting but a brief glance at the men before it disappeared into the alders at the lower end of the camp.

Ellis and Dalrymple hurried back up to the campsite. Hill and Jones arrived at the same time, and the men convened a hasty conference. Already, the light was waning. They decided that the best plan would be to take some pictures, then remove as much of the camping gear and the bodies as possible before dark. They had to deal with another safety issue as well: More bears could be heard moving through the brush, attracted by the scent of blood and gore, and the men heard an occasional popping of jaws. It would be madness to continue after dark.

Fulton left to bring his plane closer to the site, and Dalrymple and Jones set about the grisly task of digging into the cache. An occasional retching sound came from the men as more and more body parts, all female, were found. Allen Gilliland began a slow perimeter search and located more body parts. Fulton and Trooper Hill came down and found several large pieces of flesh scattered along a tunnel-like trail below the campsite. Eventually, they discovered what was left of an unidentifiable male body. Suddenly, a bear began popping its jaws not more than 15 yards away, but it was obscured by the dense tangle of brush. Gilliland kept guard, his finger curled around the trigger of his shotgun, while the other men rounded up what was left of Timothy Treadwell and hauled the parts back up to the campsite.

Three men began packing camping gear and pieces of the bodies to the planes moored in the bay, while the other three men stood guard. They were down to the last load when Trooper Hill yelled, "Bear! Bear in the area!" Ellis and Gilliland hurried to Hill's location, with Ellis standing right beside Hill, while Gilliland moved down and to his right about 10 yards.

A young bear of about 300 pounds emerged from a dense tangle of alders and stood about 30 feet away. Gilliland fired a warning shot into the ground in front of the bear, while Ellis and Hill yelled, hoping to chase the bear away. The bear moved back into the brush, then began circling the men, who had solid walls of dense brush in front of them. Intermittently, the bear appeared, then faded back into the brush. The bear's eyes unnerved Ellis. "That bear's eyes were locked on us," Ellis recalled in a later interview. "There was no fear in them. I felt it was sizing us up."

Ellis had to make a quick decision. It was almost dusk, and they still had to move back down the hill through the jungle of brush—and it was obvious that the bear was not going away. Ellis yelled for Gilliland to shoot if he could get a clear shot. Gilliland drew a bead on the bear, but the animal disappeared before he could squeeze the trigger.

Suddenly, the bear was in front of Hill and Ellis and coming fast. Joel Ellis aimed at the front of the bear's chest and fired. An instant later Hill fired, then Gilliland. The bear dropped but thrashed around, and Gilliland eased forward and put a final shot into its head. By then it was almost dark. They had no time—and no light—for the standard procedure of examining the contents of a slain bear's stomach and intestines for human remains at an attack site.

It was virtually dark when the Cessna finally lifted into the air. Joel Ellis, his mind choked with the sights of torn chunks of human flesh and the sounds of angry roars and screams of bears, picked up the receiver on the radio and called headquarters at King Salmon: "We have . . . ," his voice cracked with emotion. "We have a bear mauling to report. We have located two victims, both dead."

When Deb Liggett, who had recently transferred to the Park Service's regional office in Anchorage, heard those words crackle over the Park Service radio, she felt like a giant fist was squeezing the blood from her madly thumping heart. "I immediately thought of Timothy Treadwell," she recalled in our conversations. "But then the radio message mentioned that it was a double fatality, and I felt a wave of relief. It couldn't be Timothy because he always operated alone." Only later did Deb Liggett learn that her worst fears had indeed been realized and then some. Timothy Treadwell had taken someone along on his appointment with infamy.

The next morning, October 7, 2003, heavy rain and dense fog greeted the recovery team at the airport. Flying would be extremely dangerous. There'd been enough lives lost at Kaflia Bay. The decision was made to wait out the storm. Park officials called Jewel Palovak at Grizzly People, and she informed the next of kin. When Roland Dixon found out about the tragedy, he turned in grief and anger to his girlfriend. "Well, Timothy finally did it," he blurted. "He's been trying to get himself killed up there for years, and he finally accomplished it."

The weather cleared sufficiently on the morning of October 8 to put small aircraft in the air, and the incident team returned to Kaflia Bay. The group now included Alaska Department of Fish and Game biologist Larry Van Daele and investigator John Crye, and U.S. Fish and Wildlife Service officials Butch Patterson and Greg Wilker.

These latter four men had arrived via helicopter ahead of the Park Service team. All were armed. They immediately encountered five or six bears roaming through the brush in front of them as they moved up the hill toward the campsite. The men fired "cracker" rounds—specially made loads that explode when they hit the ground. Aimed to hit in front of approaching bears, they are designed to frighten and chase the animals away. All the bears retreated except for a large brown bear that was lying on a new food cache at the spot where the young bear had been killed. A fusillade of cracker shells finally dislodged it from the heap of dirt.

While two men dug into the damp soil at the food cache, the others moved to the place where the big red bear had been killed. Probably due to its size, estimated at a thousand pounds, and its place in the local bear hierarchy, the body had not been fed upon by other bears. Lead biologist Larry Van Daele began performing a necropsy and found the bear's stomach full of human flesh, pieces of cloth, and a T-shirt. Its large intestines also contained some human flesh.

Van Daele and his team returned to the place where the other men had been digging into the fresh cache. The young bear that had been shot was in the cache, but it had been mostly consumed by another bear. The head was intact, but only scraps of meat and bones were left on the rest of the carcass. Van Daele checked the bear's mouth and esophagus, but found no evidence of human remains. The entire team made one more sweep through the area to search for human remains that might have been missed two days earlier during the frantic search in fading light. They found nothing. They'd either done their job well the first time, or the numerous bears now roaming just out of sight in the alders had done it for them.

Bear attacks occur suddenly. The average time span between when a bear is encountered and when it attacks is only two seconds. An animal with the size and ferocity of an angry brown bear would make short work of a human. A few swats and bites and violent shakes, and it's all over. Investigators surmised that it had happened the same way with Amie Huguenard and Timothy Treadwell—that the attack had been brief, with their suffering and terror lasting but a few seconds. However, a startling discovery would make it clear that their demise was a long and torturous ordeal.

Any human death in Alaska, regardless of whether it occurs on federal land, becomes the responsibility of the state to investigate. Consequently, the material evidence from the entire Treadwell camp was turned over to state troopers as evidence. As trooper Chris Hill catalogued the gear, he came across a black plastic case that contained a video camera. Hill found a tape in the camera and popped it into a player. The video showed Timothy Treadwell advancing within an arm's reach of several bears, and Amie, in obvious discomfort, leaning away as a sow and cubs passed by just 10 feet away. The tape provided proof that, despite Treadwell's numerous letters to park officials to the contrary, he was still moving in very close to bears.

The video then goes blank, but before Hill could shut it off, the audio continued playing. Hill froze, stunned and horrified by what he heard next. For reasons unknown the camera had been turned on during the attack, with the lens cap still in place. It was initially thought that Treadwell had turned it on when he exited the tent using a remote on/off switch that he kept on his belt while in the field, but that theory was discounted after troopers found the remote switch still in the camera case. Amie, possibly at Timothy's urging, probably flipped the switch.

The audio, time coded at 1:53 P.M. on October 5, begins with Timothy's grunting and the bear growling angrily, then Treadwell's voice—loud, pleading, desperate: "Come out here! I'm being killed out here!" Followed by loud screams and the crunching of bones and gurgling gasps. Amie Huguenard then screeches, "Play dead!" More screams and growls, and then Huguenard's final plea: "Fight it!" Then Timothy Treadwell is heard for the last time, yelling in desperation, "Get a frying pan and hit it on the head!"

More guttural grunts and gasps, intermingled with screams and crunching bones and loud wailing from Huguenard. The tape does not last just a few seconds—it runs for six minutes of the most chilling, disturbing audio imaginable. Trooper Hill had nightmares for days after hearing the tape and is quoted as saying, "Believe me, you don't want to hear that tape." When the battery finally runs out after six excruciating minutes of screams and grunts and groans, Amie Huguenard is still alive and still wailing.

In the days following the tragedy, but before the tape was discovered, bear expert Barrie Gilbert, who had been severely mauled by a sow grizzly in Yellowstone National Park while doing research, was quoted as saying, "My attack happened so fast and ended so quickly, it wasn't really painful. My guess is that it happened the same way with

Treadwell and Huguenard. They probably suffered very little."
Unfortunately, the tape would prove otherwise. Treadwell and
Huguenard had not died quickly; it had been painful and it had been
terrifying. Grizzly People coordinator Jewel Palovak had her lawyer
petition the State of Alaska to keep the tape from becoming available
to the public.

CHAPTER 11

Could Bear Spray Have Saved Amie and Timothy?

People who knowingly enter bear habitat with pepper spray, guns and electric fences are committing a crime to the animals. They begin with the accepted idea of bringing instruments of pain to the animals. If they are that fearful, then they have no place in the land of this perfect animal.

> —Timothy Treadwell,
> September 14, 2003

Come out here! I'm being killed out here!. . . Hit it over the head with a frying pan!

> —Timothy Treadwell,
> October 5, 2003

Despite all that's happened, I keep coming back to the one fact, that if Timothy Treadwell had been carrying bear spray, both he and Amie and those two bears would be alive today.

> —Debra Liggett,
> Former Superintendent,
> Katmai National Park

The half-grown brown grizzly bear shuffles up through the narrow tunnel of alders and stops at the edge of a small opening to lick at a gash on his right shoulder, made just a half hour before when a bigger bear had sprung from an alder thicket and attacked it. Only the young bear's smaller size and quickness had saved its life as it outran the big bear to the alder brush tunnel.

Now, with light fading and pain and fear gripping the young bear, it limps into the opening and is startled to see a blue tent crowding the tiny clearing. A startled "huff" rumbles up from its throat. It does not turn back; the big bear could be back there. It takes a tentative step forward. "Huff! Huff!"

Suddenly, the tent flap flies open. A man steps out. "Get the hell out of here!" he yells and takes a step forward. "Get back down that trail where you came from!"

The young bear takes a step back, remembers the big bear behind it, then tries to bluff the man out of the way with two stiff hops forward while growling fiercely. But there is no place for the man to go, and he just stands there. Alders snap and pop below. The young bear rushes at the man.

The young bear leaps at the man, but an orange fog appears. The young bear is momentarily startled, then an intense pain strikes both its eyes. Blinded, it wildly paws at the air and sucks in a deep breath to bellow in rage, but the orange fog fills its lungs. The young bear can only manage a strangled, gurgling sound.

With its entire face on fire, the young bear charges blindly down through the alders. The big bear below is startled by the sudden strange noises and breaking brush and also flees. A half hour later, after burying its face in the soothing waters of an ice-cold stream, the young bear can finally see again, and the pain is almost gone. In the morning, while the young bear is resting in a thicket beside the stream, it watches the plane land, and the blond man and another human get in the plane and leave him and the other bears alone.

That's all it would have taken. One can of bear spray. Forty bucks—the price of a tank of gas.

But Timothy Treadwell wouldn't carry bear spray. He didn't want to hurt the bears.

So let's try another scenario. Suppose Amie and Tim are in their tent, gathering items for the flight out the next morning, when a bear begins huffing outside the tent. Grumbling, Timothy goes outside and yells at the bear. Sounds of scuffling and bodies thudding onto the damp grassy earth reach Amie, and Tim begins to yell for help.

Hysteria grips Amie's heart and she sits there for a second, trembling, before turning to her duffel bag. She'd been keeping a secret from Timothy. She is afraid of the bears. Actually, terrified would be a better word. But her fear is not the secret; she'd already confided that to Tim in no uncertain terms earlier in the day. Now, she frantically pulls out clothing until she gets to the bottom of the bag. Her fingers wrap around a can of bear spray, and the thought flashes through her mind, "Thank God I brought this."

Pick either one of those scenarios, and Amie Huguenard and Timothy Treadwell would probably be alive today.

Timothy Treadwell wasn't always adamantly opposed to carrying bear pepper spray. In fact, it saved his life one day. Timothy had been having a lot of problems with a subadult male brown bear he'd named Cupcake. This bear was big enough to flex its muscles and begin to assert itself in the bear hierarchy, but it was constantly bullied by the mature males. In turn, the young bear bullied lesser animals, including Timothy. Several times it had aggressively confronted him, often charging and breaking off the charge at the last moment. It got to the point where Timothy avoided being seen by the bear even from a distance.

One day, as Timothy recorded in *Among Grizzlies*, his account of his early years with the bears in Alaska, he emerged from his tent and spotted the young bear at a distance. Timothy retreated toward the safety of his tent, but the young bear had caught his scent and headed right for him. Timothy yelled at the bear, who circled the tent and then sat on some logs just 15 feet away.

As brown bears go, it was a small bear, maybe 300 pounds, but plenty big enough to tear Timothy apart. And with bears, size means everything. The bear came at Timothy, who yelled loudly and backed up against his tent, but this time the bear didn't stop. With only a second to make a decision, Timothy looked into the bear's eyes and knew that this time it would not stop.

At a distance of 5 feet, Tim blasted the bear in the face with bear spray. The bear jerked back, blinded by the red pepper, and galloped to a nearby field, where it coughed and moaned in agony while rubbing its head in the grass. Timothy was, he wrote, immediately sorry that he had hurt the bear, but when the bear charged again, "full steam," Timothy sprayed him again. Feeling that the spray alone was not enough to rout the animal, he also yelled at him and waved a stick and ended up chasing the bear for a long ways.

As he watched the young bear coughing and plunging his burning face in creek water, Timothy reflected, in *Among Grizzlies*, that he "was no longer sorry I'd sprayed Cupcake. . . . Giving him a dose of fear is exactly what he needed for his own survival." It was only later, as his reputation as a bear whisperer grew, that Treadwell announced that he would no longer carry bear spray because he didn't want to hurt the bears.

And what about an electric fence? Timothy publicly scoffed at the notion of setting up a fence barrier around his camp and often chided biologists that he encountered in the field for using them. One time he approached biologist Tom Smith and complained that Smith's camp, which was located a half-mile away from Timothy's and utilized an electric fence to keep bears away from camp, was hurting the noses of Tim's foxes and bears when they touched it.

"I informed him I was doing more of a service than he was," Tom recalls. "I also told him that by allowing the bears to roam through his camp, he was habituating them." But Timothy's refusal to even consider an electric fence may have been nothing more than bravado meant to appeal to his growing fan base. I came across a stunning letter, written by Timothy on August 2, 2000, while he was camped at Hallo Bay, to park concessionaire Becky Brock. After some small talk Timothy gets to the point: "I need the NPS [National Park Service] help. I'm trying to use an electric fence for increased safety. I can't get the current to go through the wires. The main unit works . . . [I] felt like I got sentenced to the electric chair a few times. Ouch! Could you inform your rangers to perhaps stop by when convenient and diagnose the apparatus?" This document, retrieved from Katmai National Park files under the Freedom of Information Act, proves that while Timothy may have publicly shrugged at the danger of his lifestyle, privately he was at one time or another using or attempting to use the same hot wires that he berated bear biologists for using. Becky Brock told me that she asked her rangers to stop by and help Timothy with the electric fence, but she couldn't recall where he got the electric fence from or how much he used it.

Roland Dixon, Treadwell's principal financial backer, was less than impressed by Timothy's bravado regarding bear defense products. "I told him that he should at least be carrying bear spray. I told him if he went without it I'd hold back the financing, and he'd always say okay, but then I'd read a quote from him that carrying bear spray was contrary to the message he was trying to bring to the bears."

Treadwell's idiosyncrasies were one issue, but placing another person's life in jeopardy gets Dixon fuming: "I told him under no circumstances could he take [Amie] up there. I threatened to pull his financing if he did. I told him he should listen to Charlie Russell and carry bear spray and string an electric fence around his camp. He said okay to all of it, but he never did any of it. It was immoral what he did with that poor girl. There's no way she knew what she was getting herself into."

Mark Matheny, owner of Universal Defense Alternative Products (UDAP) and maker of Pepper Power bear spray, makes a couple of trips to Alaska each year, partly because he loves the land and the people, but also to educate folks about the value of carrying bear spray and to encourage people to carry it when they recreate. Mark says that a bear attack is no fun, and he should know. While hiking along a ridge trail in Montana's Gallatin National Forest north of Yellowstone National Park, he once stumbled upon a female grizzly with two cubs feeding on a cow elk carcass. The bear slammed into Mark and tore at his face. She took his head in her jaws and bit down so hard that Mark thought his head would explode. The bite left a divot in the top of his head that could cradle a golf ball.

Fortunately, his companion, Fred Bohnson, carried a small can of personal defense pepper spray, but when he advanced toward the bear, she turned on him, swatted the spray from his hand, and bit him several times before returning to again savage Mark. Though hurt and bleeding, Fred retrieved the can of pepper spray, and when the bear turned on him again, he sprayed her in the face. The bear jerked her head back, pawed at her face, and charged off into the forest with her cubs.

Mark went about designing a more potent bear spray that would be EPA approved. In the past irresponsible profit seekers have marketed cheap, low-quality pepper spray as bear spray. That's when the EPA stepped in and required any manufacturer who labeled its product "bear spray" to meet minimum capsaicin (rendered red pepper that is concentrated) levels with sufficient propellant to get the spray out there quickly. Mark's bear spray shoots out an oil-based fog of red-hot pepper 30 feet long and 15 feet wide in a microsecond. Currently, six manufacturers produce EPA-approved bear spray.

Mark's been marketing his bear spray with the zeal of a biblical prophet for more than fifteen years. "Bear spray is really catching on in Alaska," he told me, "but it took a few years to convince the guys who'd just say they have a gun to stop aggressive bears. Now, a lot of them are carrying bear spray."

In fairness to those skeptical Alaskans, it is hard to believe that a can of bear spray could stop an animal as enormous as a half-ton brown bear, especially when a fusillade of bullets sometimes fails to stop a charging brownie. Alaskan Dale Bagley found that out one balmy April morning when he went scouting for a new moose-hunting area along the Killey River for the fall hunt. Dale spent the better part of the morning looking over the country and checking for tracks at river crossings. While walking past a brush thicket, he heard some ravens croaking. Black bear season was open, and he had a bear hunting license, so he thought he'd ease over in the direction of the sounds and see if a black bear was feeding on a carcass.

Then he got cold feet. Maybe, he thought, it's a grizzly. So he started circling around the thicket. He walked right into a large bear, which stood 60 feet away. Dale identified it as a grizzly, and he could see the moose carcass it had been feeding on. Dale wasn't too concerned because he possessed plenty of firepower. He carried a semi automatic 30.06 rifle loaded with 220-grain slugs, and he had a .44 magnum pistol on his hip.

Dale didn't know what to do, so he started yelling at the bear. The bear didn't react. It just sat there while Dale backed away, the rifle in his left hand, the pistol in his right hand. Then he fired a shot into the air to further discourage the bear from charging. It didn't look like the bear was going to charge, so Dale put the pistol in its holster. An instant later, the bear charged, coming low and fast. He threw the rifle to his shoulder and looked through the scope, but all he could see was hair, so he fired. The bear stopped like it had hit a brick wall, but then it was coming at him again. Dale squeezed the trigger again, but the gun misfired, so he pulled out his pistol and fired an instant before the bear slammed into him.

The bear bit his face and head, but the bear's weight, estimated at 800 pounds, kept the pistol pinned to Dale's chest. Dale endured several more crushing bites to his head before he could free his hand. He shoved the pistol into the bear's belly and pulled the trigger. The bear grunted but kept biting. So Dale fired again, and again and again. The bear staggered backward and ran off. Dale's head and face were torn badly and he was bleeding profusely, but he was able to stagger back to his truck, and a good Samaritan rushed him to the hospital.

Fred Woods had the same problem stopping a charging bear with a gun. Fred is the host of the Portland, Oregon, television program *Northwest Hunter*. When Fred went hunting for brown bears in Alaska, his choice of firearm was a .416 Remington magnum, whose 400-grain bullet and case resembles a small mortar shell. One day he spotted a big brown bear 200 yards away, so he laid the crosshairs on the bear's shoulder and squeezed the trigger. The bear went down but got up. Fred shot again. The bear went down but got up. This went on for three more shots until the bear finally piled up less than 10 feet from Fred.

Fred began investigating bear spray as an alternative just in case a grizzly jumped out of the brush at close range. He told me during an interview, "I knew from personal experience that if you don't kill a grizzly immediately, shooting it some more only increases its rage. I chose bear pepper spray as an alternative because I became convinced that it canceled that rage factor."

When Fred strapped on his bear spray during an Alaskan caribou hunt, he drew a few chuckles and snide remarks like: "What's that, flavoring for the bear? Ha! Ha!" But that afternoon Fred had the last laugh when he and another hunter went out with the guide to scout for caribou. They located a sizable herd across a river, but since it was so late in the day, they decided to go back to camp and take up the hunt in the morning. As they approached camp, Fred was in the lead. When the men came around the front of the first tent, a brown bear cub ran away squealing. A second later a huge female brown bear exploded out of the tent 30 feet away and charged. While the other men frantically struggled to get their rifles to their shoulders, Fred pulled out his bear spray and blasted the bear at 20 feet. The bear skidded to a halt, pawing at the orange fog that had enveloped it, then swapped ends and galloped away with her cub.

"That's the problem with a rifle," Fred cautions. "If you surprise a bear like that, you don't have time to unsling your rifle." Studies of bear attacks that occurred when a bear was surprised at close range, which accounts for 90 percent of all bear attacks, lend credence to Fred's admonition. The average time an attacking bear takes to get to the human is 1.9 seconds.

Everyone knows that bears are smart, but the level of their intelligence surprises even knowledgeable bear people. And nothing prompts a bear's craftiness like the allure of food. In the fall when the bears are ravenously devouring any food in preparation for hibernation, they have been known to follow the sounds of gunfire because they've learned that a reward in the form of a carcass or gut pile will result.

Unfortunately, the hunter is sometimes still present at the carcass, and fatalities have resulted. Two British Columbia hunters who were field dressing a six-point bull elk in knee-deep snow were attacked and killed by a female grizzly. The men's guns were safely stored a distance from the carcass. And in Montana in November 2002, Timothy Hillston was mauled and killed by a female grizzly bear while he field dressed a cow elk in the Blackfoot-Clearwater Wildlife Management Area, 38 miles northeast of Missoula. Hillston was surprised while he gutted the elk, and he may have tried to get off a shot. His rifle was lying on the ground with the bolt open. Hillston was not killed immediately by the bear. He crawled a distance before expiring.

Most hunters take extreme care of their firearms, and they often unload them and place them a safe distance from the kill site. This action puts them at the mercy of an opportunistic bear. As a result, the Montana Department of Fish, Wildlife, and Parks has added a notice in their hunting regulations that all hunters in bear country should also carry bear spray and keep it on their belt when taking care of a downed animal.

I frequently lecture on the subject of bear avoidance and defense. I've also sprayed two bears and a mountain lion with bear spray, and each time the animals immediately ceased their aggressive actions and left the area. And when I was writing my book *True Stories of Bear Attacks: Who Survived and Why*, I interviewed thirty-five people who had sprayed attacking bears and stopped them in their tracks.

Despite overwhelming evidence that bear spray deters aggressive bears, many people, I was frustrated to find out, still doubted its potency. I certainly couldn't go to the bears and ask them how they felt after being sprayed, so in a moment of weakness (or perhaps it was madness?), I hatched a plan. I would rush at a friend, low like a bear, with news cameras rolling to show how bear spray worked.

On a sunny spring morning in Bozeman, Montana, 40 yards separated me from a man standing with a can of bear spray on his hip. I rushed at him, and as I closed in, I remember seeing a beautiful orange cloud coming out to meet me. The next moment I was writhing on the ground, coughing, snorting, hacking, even farting! The plan was for me to speak to the camera and explain the spray's effects, but all that was forgotten. I was in survival mode. My lungs burned like fire, and my eyes felt like someone was jabbing them with needles. Fortunately, soap and water was handy, and I was able to wash off most of the red pepper. Though I endured pain and misery for a half hour, the effects eased quickly. Within the hour I was having lunch. Television stations ran this film segment across the West, and I became known as "the crazy guy who let himself get sprayed with bear spray." Many thousands of viewers, however, were able to see first-hand how bear spray works.

Bear pepper spray is now accepted by professional bear biologists as a bear deterrent. The Interagency Grizzly Bear Committee (IGBC) has issued a position paper on bear pepper spray, prepared by the Center for Wildlife Information. The purpose of the paper is to set guidelines based on both scientific research and reports from wildlife specialists who have used bear pepper spray during encounters. The theme of the paper states,: "While bear pepper spray is not a substitute for following proper bear avoidance safety techniques, bear spray has been used successfully in a variety of confrontations with grizzly bears."

Bear expert Tom Smith is also an outspoken proponent of bear spray. "The facts are real clear on pepper spray," Tom said in an *Alaska* magazine article. "It's not a real debatable issue. It's got probably the best safety record of all the defense measures out there."

Smith's research on the use of firearms during a bear attack indicates a large percentage of people using guns for defense experience injuries during a bear attack. Smith thinks that the difficulty of unslinging a firearm then taking careful aim at a charging bear and hitting it in a vital area may be the reason for the rise in injuries. (Remember, most bear attacks occur when a bear is surprised at close range, and the average response time is only about two seconds.) Conversely, bear spray such as UDAP can be shot from the hip, and most EPA-approved bear sprays shoot a loud blast of dense red-pepper concentrate in a fog that can spread 30 feet outward and 15 feet wide. So even during the hectic few seconds while a bear is charging, most people are capable of hitting a charging bear in the face with the spray.

Tom Smith is driven absolutely crazy when he hears a hair-raising story about a near-disastrous encounter between an aggressive bear and a person who is not carrying bear spray. Such an incident occurred, Tom reported to me, in Denali National Park in August 2000 between a seasonal park ranger and a predatory black bear. It typifies the grave risk that is taken by unprepared people in bear country.

Ranger Carlin Kaufman was on routine trail patrol along the McKinley Bar trail near Wonder Lake when she began hearing sounds behind her. But each time she checked her back trail, she saw nothing. Then she heard another noise behind her and turned to find a very large black bear galloping at her. Carlin yelled and waved her arms, and the bear stopped and circled her. She began throwing rocks at the bear and several times saw the dust fly from the bear's fur when a rock found its mark. But the bear kept coming—stalking her, snarling, and showing its teeth.

Carlin was terrified and began swinging her radio at the bear. Twice she bounced the radio off the bear's head and backed it off, but each time it returned, more brazen than ever. One time it advanced to just a few feet away from her. "I was absolutely terrified while all this was happening. It seemed like an eternity that I was fending this bear off [it was actually thirty minutes]. At one point it looked like I'd get mauled for sure, and when I looked at those huge teeth snarling at me, I thought, 'Boy, this is going to hurt really bad.'"

Then Carlin had an idea: She turned her radio to full volume and turned up the squelch. The instant the loud, piercing static ripped through the air, the bear ran off. When Tom Smith asked Carlin why she wasn't at least carrying bear spray, she timidly replied, "Well, there weren't supposed to be a lot of bears in the area."

"That girl went through hell for a half hour," Tom fumes, "and she came very close to being mauled. The entire incident could have been avoided if she'd been carrying bear spray. And that predatory bear would have gotten a good dose of aversive conditioning that would make it think twice the next time it encountered a human."

Tom Smith has become so convinced that bear spray should be carried by travelers in bear country in our national parks and forests that he arranged to have bear spray manufacturer Mark Matheny and me speak to a select audience of federal and state land managers on the subject of bear spray in Anchorage on June 21, 2004.

Amazingly, some people don't carry bear spray because they don't want to hurt the animal. People who carry bear spray don't want to hurt bears, either. They want to save them. Blasting a bear with a snoot full of bear spray furnishes it a healthy dose of aversive conditioning. True, that bear's first impulse may be to avoid the next human it encounters. But is that so bad?

Timothy Treadwell thought so, and he mentioned that as the reason that he stopped carrying pepper spray, despite the fact that it had saved his life when the young male bear attacked him at his tent. In typical "bear whisperer" fashion, he explained, "Doesn't seem fair to the bears. Why should they suffer because of me?" An interesting statement, and a complete change of tune from the statements he had made in *Among Grizzlies*. Timothy said in his book that he was glad he'd sprayed the young bear and that giving it a dose of fear was exactly what the aggressive teenager needed for his future survival. It is also worth noting that Timothy never again mentioned being harassed by that bear.

But what about Amie Huguenard? Had Timothy forbidden her to bring bear spray to the Grizzly Maze? Or had she bravely declined to carry it in deference to his assurance that as long as she was with him she'd be safe? During a Discovery Channel television program, Timothy had admitted that "[if] anyone tries to do what I do, they will get hurt." That statement would seem to contradict an assurance that Amie would stay safe if she stuck with him. Plus, we know that Amie wasn't always at Timothy's side. The video found after their deaths showed that Timothy had left Amie by herself. He filmed her at a distance, and she was obviously uncomfortable and leaning away as massive bears walked stiffly past her.

Tragically and ironically, staying *beside* Timothy Treadwell outside the tent that day is the choice that led to Amie Huguenard's death.

I'm a bear lover and a member of the Great Bear Foundation. I love black bears, grizzly bears, brown bears, and polar bears. And I love being in bear country. I doubt that Timothy Treadwell was any more fond of bears than I am. Yet I've sprayed two bears with bear spray. I hurt them; something Timothy said he'd never do to a bear. But neither have I ever killed a grizzly. Yet Timothy was responsible for the deaths of those two brown grizzly bears at the site of the tragedy, just as surely as if he'd pulled the trigger instead of leaving that horrid business to investigators Allen Gilliland, Derek Dalrymple, and Joel Ellis.

CHAPTER 12

Who Killed Timothy Treadwell?

WHO KILLED TIMOTHY TREADWELL? That's an easy one. The bears did it. They finally showed their true colors and killed their savior and protector on the afternoon of October 5, 2003. Small wonder, some might say, that our grandpas and their grandpas shot, trapped, and poisoned the dang things into near extinction in the lower forty-eight states. One can only hope that Canada and Alaska will finally get up to speed and eradicate the rest of those monsters before they start roaming the streets of Anchorage, snatching babies from their mother's arms.

Unfortunately, those sentiments represent the opinion of the majority of people I talk to about grizzly bears. They're afraid of them, to the point of hysteria, and Timothy Treadwell's death only strengthened their resolve that the grizzly bear is a menace and inherently dangerous to any human it encounters.

That's why Timothy Treadwell's death is such a tragedy. Beyond the tearful, poetic eulogies of his followers lies the grave of a man who died a horrible death, torn apart and eaten by the same bears he'd been telling the world were mild, affectionate creatures. The purpose of this book, from its inception in my head through every single page, has been to make sure this tragedy is not repeated. I am strongly convinced that this tragedy could have, and should have, been prevented. Accountability is required. To ignore this issue would invite history to repeat itself.

Some bears are killers. In this dubious category bears and humans are indeed very much alike. For whatever reason a very small percentage of humans and bears are capable of malevolent metamorphoses that can change their basic nature from benign to hostile. Criminal analysts suggest that maybe one person in 40,000 is capable of murder. Curiously, that statistic also applies quite accurately to bears. In the state of Alaska, which harbors about 40,000 grizzlies, maybe one bear out of that total number will show a predatory tendency toward a human being.

The half-dozen bear attacks that occur in Alaska annually are rarely predatory. More often than not, a grizzly attack is defensive-aggressive, meaning that the bear feels threatened by the sudden appearance of a human within its safety zone (60 yards) and rushes forward to swat or shake its adversary before fleeing.

One certainly couldn't call the bear that killed Vitaly Nikolaenko predatory. Over the course of several days, Nikolaenko literally stalked the poor animal through deep snow, several times moving close enough to provoke a charge. And still the bear was reluctant to attack his tormentor. Finally, cornered in a thicket and terrified of the man who continued pressing it, the bear attacked from a distance of only 10 feet and killed Nikolaenko before galloping up the mountain to den for the winter.

Neither could one call the bear that killed Timothy Treadwell predatory. Kaflia Bay is a small place, and Timothy was all over it. He'd pestered every bear enough for each animal to know who he was and where he was. If the bear that killed Amie and Timothy had been predatory, investigators would have read about it in Tim's diary: losing its instinctive fear of humans, acting aggressive, stalking, etc. The bear that killed Timothy and Amie was—again, my opinion—a subadult who felt threatened by the sudden appearance of Tim screaming in its face. To say that this bear was responsible for Timothy Treadwell's death is akin to saying that a car is responsible for the death of a jay-walking pedestrian.

If the bears didn't kill Timothy Treadwell, then who did? The consensus opinion among knowledgeable bear people is that Timothy killed himself. The evidence weighs heavily in that direction. Hadn't he, at various times during his career, proclaimed the belief that he'd probably be killed by a bear? And hadn't he stated publicly that he wanted to end his life that way? What else is there to think about a guy who says it would be an honor to end up as bear shit?

The vast majority of people on the street, however, simply believe that Timothy Treadwell was not in his right mind. Even interviewer Keith Morrison grew frustrated enough with Timothy during his *Dateline NBC* special "Gentle Tim" that he blurted, "This is crazy! This is nuts! These bears can break you in half like a match stick."

To which Timothy, beaming at the intensity of Morrison's question, calmly replied, "I believe they're misunderstood." Only later, on the rainswept knoll in the Grizzly Maze, would Timothy learn the harsh truth of that statement.

Ample proof of instability in Timothy Treadwell can be collected easily. How sane can a guy be when he lopes around on all fours like a bear in front of chagrined biologists and frightened tourists? What would anyone think when they saw this strange man on all fours beside a bear, lapping water with his tongue or splashing at the water with his hands—just as a bear would do? These may be the types of disturbing videotaped antics that Grizzly People has tucked away in its archives, videos that were recalled by Treadwell's chief financial benefactor Roland Dixon. But mental illness was not at the heart of Timothy Treadwell's tragic demise. He was lucid, articulate, nondelusional, and fully capable of understanding the world around him, even if he did filter it to conform to his preconceived ideals. Timothy may have had emotional problems, but he wasn't nuts.

Neither was Timothy Treadwell suicidal, as we learned from the audio recovered at the tragedy site. That tape recorded Timothy begging the woman of his life to leave the safety of the tent and save him because he was being killed. He pleaded with Amie to hit the bear over the head with a frying pan. Both requests amounted to a death sentence for Amie Huguenard.

Roland Dixon is, to my knowledge, the only Treadwell supporter who counseled him to stop getting so close to the bears. Others must have seen the manic desire for the confrontation and the adrenaline reward. Surely someone in that tight-knit corps of animal rights, eco-warrior environmental organizations that Timothy was associated with—Grizzly People, Sea Shepherd, Environment Now, Last Chance for Animals, Natural Resource Defense Council—must have murmured at some point, "Gee, he's gonna get himself killed if he keeps doing stuff like that."

Timothy Treadwell simply could not help himself, in the beginning or the end. Even after fame and impending fortune arrived, he was inexorably drawn to the bears. It remained for his friends to help him grow beyond his fixation with the tauntingly close bear encounter.

Instead, Timothy's weakness was misread as genius. Using the term "magical" ad nauseam to describe his personality only served to fuel Timothy's desire for recognition, and when the "bear whisperer" moniker was laid on him, Timothy Treadwell became a casualty of his fame. A year before Tim's death, Chuck Bartlebaugh had painstakingly laid out for him a plan to make Timothy a national spokesman for sensible stewardship and responsible actions around bears, but Timothy wasn't interested. Stewardship or bear whisperer. The choice wasn't even close. Timothy chose the glamour and ran with it.

Were the very people who claimed Timothy Treadwell as their hero responsible for his death? No, but they did nothing to stop it, either.

One entity that used Timothy Treadwell without regard for his life was Hollywood, that amalgamation of television networks, outdoor adventure channels, and investigative programs that are as obsessed with finding a good story as Timothy was with confronting brown bears. Timothy's activities and his personality were a perfect fit for television exploitation, beginning with the *Tom Snyder Show* and escalating to *Late Night with David Letterman*.

I have tapes of all of Timothy's television programs, and I am filled with frustration and outrage when I watch program hosts such as Tom Snyder and Stone Phillips hail Timothy as a bear-man who holds special powers over the animals. They showed film clips of Timothy moving within feet of brown bears—singing love songs to them, reading to them, touching them—and they never bothered to ask any recognized bear biologists if this type of activity was condoned among professionals. They never investigated the legitimacy of Timothy's research or the legality of Timothy's actions.

I greatly admire Stone Phillips, but he must have taken the day off when he introduced the *Dateline NBC* program "Gentle Tim." Phillips begins with the words, "Usually when we hear about the mighty grizzly, it's about a harrowing grizzly bear attack. But is that typical? A man you're about to meet says no. In fact, he says grizzly bears are really gentle giants, and to prove it he lives with them. He also talks and sings to them and crawls with them. He's part Doctor Doolittle and part Grizzly Adams. . ." Whereupon Timothy comes onscreen and breaks just about every bear rule in Katmai National Park.

Timothy Treadwell's national exposure as the bear-whispering savior and protector of grizzlies was not limited solely to television. While Treadwell was alive, the Audubon Society decided to make a video featuring Timothy Treadwell. The producer of the film contacted respected bear biologist Sterling Miller and two other Alaska biologists and asked them to lend their expertise to the endeavor by checking the script for accuracy. The three men conferred and marked up the script before returning it. Sterling told me, "They had a lot of stuff in there with Timothy moving in close to bears and protecting the bears from poachers, so we crossed them out, but the script came back to us with that stuff still in it, so we crossed it out again and sent it back, but it came back with that nonsense still in it."

Finally, the producer called and asked Sterling what they should do with the script. "I told him that in our opinions, it was an inaccurate, distorted script that supported the dangerous practice of moving in too close to bears. The producer said thanks and hung up. I learned later that they produced the video anyway."

Even after Timothy's death television program producers continue to probe for kernels of sensationalism. Biologist Tom Smith told me that a few months after Timothy was killed, the Discovery Channel interviewed him about bears for an upcoming program. The producer asked Tom a few mundane questions about a brown bear's size and weight, then he blurted, "Isn't it true that Timothy Treadwell was killed by a dominant male because he had assimilated himself into the bear world's hierarchy, and the big bear killed him because he felt competition?"

"I told him that Timothy had his bears all wrong," Tom recalls. "They're not people in bear uniforms, and Tim Treadwell never was a bear in a human uniform."

Hollywood aided and abetted the demise of Timothy Treadwell, but it has an opportunity to redeem itself. Movie star Leonardo DiCaprio has teamed with Columbia Pictures to produce a feature film about Timothy Treadwell's life. The film is scheduled for release in 2005 or 2006 and will be called *The Man Who Loved Grizzlies*. Since DiCaprio supported Timothy financially, it will be interesting to see if this movie promotes the "magic" of Timothy the bear whisperer, or chooses biological accuracy instead. Don't bet the farm on the latter.

Without an outlet for his outlandish filmed sequences, Timothy would have been forced to take a different path toward recognition and legitimacy. A scientific approach to legitimate research-driven fame would have taken a bit longer, but had he taken that route, Timothy might be alive today, a crusader for good stewardship in bear country. But Timothy followed the bright lights. Now he's dead, just like other bright-burning stars who took a similar path to celebrity, only to have their flame suddenly extinguished.

Of course, without sensationalistic footage of Timothy close to bears, Hollywood wouldn't have given him the time of day. In other words, without close-ups of Timothy standing 10 feet away from a bear and crooning, "I love you, Tabitha," there would have been no national television exposure. No television exposure, no cult following, no bear whisperer, perhaps no Grizzly People.

Which leads to the core of the debate over who killed Timothy Treadwell. Whoever allowed Timothy to move in close to those bears enabled him to commit his illegal actions. I would say that no national park or wildlife refuge in the lower forty-eight states would have allowed Timothy to engage in the activities he did at Katmai—for a dozen years. Yellowstone? Forget it! Its rangers would have been on Tim in a heartbeat and ushered him out of the park. Glacier? The rangers there are even stricter, but so are the bears. Timothy wouldn't have made it past his first grizzly lovefest.

Alaska is no easy touch, either. Denali National Park exerts total control over its visitors. If you want a motor tour of the park, plan on boarding a park bus. Campers need to apply for a camping permit and then are required to attend a half-hour wildlife safety indoctrination before they're issued a permit—just to camp overnight.

So what happened in Katmai National Park? What atmosphere existed that would allow Timothy Treadwell to repeatedly and flagrantly break park rules against moving too close to the bears for twelve years without receiving a ticket?

When Katmai National Park's bear-viewing potential was discovered in the late 1980s, park officials were anxious to help Alaskan commercial outfitters who poured into the park. Unlike Denali, which has a road system running through the heart of it, thereby allowing most tourists to visit the park without an outfitter, Katmai is roadless. The vast majority of tourists at Katmai are served by commercial outfitters who offer their services via plane or boat for fishing and bear viewing. When Timothy Treadwell arrived in 1989, he discovered a friendly "let's all just get along" relationship between the commercial outfitters and park personnel. In fairness to Katmai rangers, it must be conceded that they were not accustomed to dealing with individual tourists. Their reluctance to exert heavy-handed treatment of this strange bear-man was understandable. But when officials became aware, through Treadwell's book, *Among Grizzlies*, that he was regularly violating park rules each season, they should have ejected him from the park. Regulations for safe distances between bears and humans had been continually disregarded, as the book and subsequent films proved.

The failure of the solicitor's office to recommend prosecution and eviction of Timothy Treadwell even after Deb Liggett showed them the shockingly close bear encounters on videotape set in motion an attitude of tolerance. Even the home page of the Grizzly People Web site shows Timothy smiling at the camera with a stiff-legged, stressed-out brown bear eyeing him just 20 yards away. Still, Katmai staff and legal counsel took no action.

Rangers who were already accustomed to "getting along" with bear-viewing contractors demonstrated more than just enormous restraint toward Timothy; they essentially befriended him. Friends don't give friends tickets, one might quip. Timothy's letters to female park personnel are almost embarrassing to read, and they remain fodder for those people who contend that he was a wily manipulator who used the Katmai rangers to get his way.

But no matter how exceptional the circumstances, how endearing this goofy oddball was, at some point the ship should have been righted. Park personnel are entrusted with the duty to protect the land, its wildlife, and the people who visit it. They failed miserably in all three categories. Hallo Bay and Kaflia Bay became the settings for several nature "documentary" films—all of which documented the clear disregard for park rules. This situation led to the deaths of two bears and two humans.

As required by park rules, a Technical Board of Investigation into the deaths of Amie Huguenard and Timothy Treadwell was convened to review the incident. Their investigation included all circumstances of the incident, park responses, and factors contributing to the fatalities.

Katmai National Park had been severely criticized through the years by respected bear biologists, and by Center for Wildlife Information director Chuck Bartlebaugh in a letter to park superintendent Deb Liggett, for allowing Timothy Treadwell free rein within its boundaries. One might think that the Technical Board's investigation for the National Park Service would bring together a group of international bear experts and park policy managers from Washington, D.C., to address the issue of bear and visitor safety. Instead, four of the five board members were Katmai National Park employees.

The board chairman was Joe Fowler, superintendent of Katmai National Park. Other board members were Missy Epping, acting chief ranger at Katmai; Tammy Olson, wildlife biologist at Katmai; Roy Wood, chief of interpretation at Katmai; and Larry Van Daele, area wildlife biologist from the Alaska Department of Fish and Game.

The board listened to testimony by ranger Joel Ellis, who was the operations chief during the emergency response effort. They then heard from Larry Van Daele regarding the contents of the videotape recovered at the incident site. The board then issued a list of findings and contributing factors surrounding the incident.

Among the most prominent findings: The audiotape indicates that after Treadwell was attacked, Huguenard was alive for at least six minutes. Then the camera battery runs out. It is unknown how much time actually elapsed between the attack on Treadwell and Huguenard's death. Another finding was that the large male bear killed near the campsite had human remains in its stomach. It was estimated to be 1,000 pounds and twenty-eight years old. It appeared to be in reasonable conditions for a bear its age, with well-worn teeth and broken canines, but it had no signs of obvious injury and had abundant rump fat for hibernation. This bear had been tagged fifteen years earlier in nearby Kukak Bay and had the number 141 tattooed on the inside of its lower lip. A third finding was that Treadwell had a long history of engaging in behavior that is considered dangerous while bear viewing and camping on the Katmai Coast. Last among the most prominent findings was that Treadwell had publicly acknowledged the risk he was taking and advised others not to engage in similar behavior.

The contributing factors identified by the Technical Board of Investigation included one that stated that the location of the campsite was a primary factor leading to the bear confrontation that resulted in the deaths of Treadwell and Huguenard. The camp location was near active salmon-spawning areas, at the convergence of several well-used bear trails, and in an area of bear day beds. These factors made close contact with the bears likely at the campsite.

Another of the contributing factors in Treadwell's death was his pattern of occupying prime feeding sites where bears congregate along the Katmai Coast. His decision to camp at that particular site during a time of year when the bears were fiercely competing for food matched his typical pattern, the report concluded, and contributed to his death. The board also found that a small amount of food was stored in Treadwell's sleep tent. Undisturbed by bears, the food included cheese and sausage in a resealable plastic bag, an open bag of chips, and a candy bar. Bundling together the facts and patterns, the contributing factors also included a statement that it was possible that bears investigated the camp in part due to the food found in the sleeping tent, and that the fatal confrontation resulted as a consequence of Treadwell's history of approaching bears and allowing bears to approach him within a few feet.

The board ended its investigation with the following conclusions: Treadwell and Huguenard died from a bear attack that might have been avoided by adhering to basic principles of camping in bear country. Establishing their camp away from obvious bear travel ways and known feeding areas likely would have prevented the confrontation that resulted in their deaths. Though their camp did not violate park regulations, it was established contrary to precautions well known to Treadwell. In addition, the patterns of behavior exhibited by Treadwell appeared to be a result of his opinion that he had established a special relationship with the bears in the area of the camp. This pattern of behavior is well documented on video taken by Treadwell and presented to the public by several national media outlets.

The Technical Board of Investigation, comprised and headed by Katmai National Park officials, then tackled the touchy subject of whether any act or omission by the National Park Service (NPS) was a contributing factor in the incident. The board determined that, given Treadwell's history of activity in Katmai and park staff interactions with him, no additional information or warnings from the park staff would have influenced the outcome.

In other words the board decided that, despite the fact that two people were dead and two bears killed, they wouldn't have changed a single detail of NPS involvement in the tragedy. Despite the fact that Timothy Treadwell had repeatedly violated park policy by moving too close to bears for thirteen years, he was never issued a single citation. Despite the fact that Treadwell often appeared on prime-time television programs moving within mere feet of bears, the park staff felt no obligation to evict him. Despite the fact that Treadwell had literally lived for months at a time in the midst of bears year after year in Hallo Bay and Kaflia Bay, the park felt no responsibility to intervene on behalf of the well-being of the bears or the safety of a human being who obviously needed protection—if not from the bears, then from himself.

Of course, the board also called for the standard comprehensive review of Katmai's management procedures and policies, but little has been changed to avoid future tragedies of this type. Already, a fresh wave of visitors intent on repeating Treadwell's patterns has arrived at the cordial coast of Katmai National Park. Officials admit that as many as four individuals may be operating in a questionable manner within park boundaries. They do say that some of these individuals have been warned and cited. Perhaps the staff *has* learned the wisdom of a cautious, firm approach to its visitors.

Visitor Andreas Kieling, for instance, was cited by Katmai Park rangers for a fishing violation. He then received a warning for moving too close to the bears. Finally, he was cited for violating the 50/100 yard rule. In spite of this record, however, park officials did not eject Kieling. In June 2004 Kieling starred in an *Animal Planet* segment called "Grizzly Encounter."

My own conclusion is that no single factor is responsible for Timothy Treadwell's death. Most certainly, the lax enforcement of regulations and a convivial staff-visitor attitude at Katmai was a huge factor. So also was the unrealistic, unscientific, and questionable support of the eco-warrior groups and individuals who cheered when Timothy risked death repeatedly.

But the one factor that played the largest part in this tragedy was the man himself. Timothy Treadwell may have suffered from bipolar disorder or from other neurological deficiencies that may have altered his reasoning power to a degree, but not permanently. Evidence supports huge blocks of time when Timothy was lucid and perceptive—and therefore responsible for his actions. During the television program *Grizzly Diaries*, Timothy reminds viewers, "If people try to do what I do, they will get hurt." And in the Epilogue of his book, *Among Grizzlies*, he writes, "It is my greatest fear that some people might attempt to copy my past dangerous style of study and become injured or killed."

Timothy Treadwell set out with an agenda, and no matter how much he was spurred on by fanatical admirers or facilitated by chummy park rangers or ratings-driven television producers, it remained for the man to act responsibly. He did not. His reckless actions caused his death. They killed both the woman who loved him and two bears he swore to protect.

CHAPTER 13

The Treadwell Legacy

ANYONE WHO THOUGHT THEY heard the last of Timothy Treadwell after he died was mistaken. In the days and weeks following his death, newspaper and magazine articles and readers' responses flooded the media. Opinions varied greatly. After the *Los Angeles Times* published an in-depth feature on Treadwell, they received a mixed bag of reactions from readers.

An anti-Treadwell letter reads:

The story behind the fatal mauling of "adventurer" Timothy Treadwell and Amie Huguenard by grizzly bears is another sad consequence of the self-serving "I've got to be me" attitude hanging around from the late '60s. Treadwell's selfishness and lack of genuine respect for wildlife resulted in his death, the death of his girlfriend, a grave risk to the rangers who retrieved their remains, and the shooting of two of the beloved grizzlies that Treadwell claimed were giving purpose to his—and only his—life.

That one was followed by a pro-Treadwell letter:

I first met Timothy Treadwell when he came to my third-grade class in 1999 and gave his grizzly bear presentation, which taught the students about Alaska, grizzly bears, and the ecosystem. He encouraged students to study hard, stay in school, and stay off drugs. Timothy was a rare individual. His burning desire to help animals was not limited to grizzly bears. In the spring he was also involved with saving harp seals from slaughter. Please keep in mind that besides photographing the bears, Timothy was also defending them from poachers.

Another reader is not bothered by the deaths of people but by the loss of the bears:

> I am appalled at the poor judgment of the park rangers and state troopers in their killing of two bears while they were recovering the remains of Treadwell and his girlfriend, Amie Huguenard. If these supposed professionals are incapable of better management of animals, they shouldn't be allowed out in the wild with guns. There was clearly no danger to human beings beyond that caused by the actions of the people who killed the bears. Any "immediate threat" to their lives was of their own creation. Furthermore, the death of the animals compounds the tragedy of the human deaths. One suspects that Treadwell would have preferred his remains be left where they were rather than a recovery attempt resulting in the deaths of these magnificent animals he loved.

This person obviously forgot that when the rangers were charged by the big, red-colored, half-ton brown bear, they still were acting under the assumption that they were on a rescue mission, not a body-parts pick up.

The most enlightening letter came from a former Katmai Park manager, G. Ray Bane of Kula, Hawaii:

> The story of Timothy Treadwell and his friend's deaths in Katmai National Park was a tragedy for all concerned, including the bears. I served as superintendent at Katmai from 1987 to 1992 and am familiar with the location and circumstances of the event. Treadwell knowingly violated basic rules of respecting and observing wildlife in the park. He placed his campsite at the bear feeding site and kept it in place for a long period, resulting in the accumulation of food odors. Katmai bears in the fall are driven by a need to put on as much bulk as possible before entering their winter dens. He apparently believed that he was somehow exempt from hostile reactions of the bears and frequently moved in close to them.
>
> This is not only personally foolish, but it also habituates the bears to reducing their normal tendency to avoid close human contact. Treadwell may have convinced himself and others that he was a modern version of "Grizzly Adams," but he ultimately caused the deaths of his friend and two park bears, plus possibly endangering other people and bears by his actions.

I did my own informal Timothy Treadwell public-opinion survey in June 2004. Not in Malibu or Los Angeles, but in Kodiak, Alaska. This port city of 3,000—the seventh-largest municipality in Alaska—is located on Kodiak Island and was the staging ground for Timothy's excursions into Katmai, most recently using Andrew Airways for the half-hour floatplane flight to Hallo Bay or Kaflia Bay.

For several days I walked the same streets where Timothy had supposedly become a fixture and had confronted all the hunters. I chatted about the weather with people I met, and I asked about Timothy Treadwell. The response was surprising since Kodiak had been Timothy's staging ground for his expeditions into Katmai National Park for thirteen years. "Who?" was the reaction of half the people. But after I explained who Timothy was and what he did, they scoffed, "Oh, that's just nuts! Why would anyone in their right mind do something like that?"

Of the people I encountered in Kodiak who knew who Timothy Treadwell was, nine out of ten were against him for a variety of reasons. The most common complaint was that he was a Californian who, "like the rest of them down there," tried to push his scatterbrained ideas about bears on Alaskans who are, by the way, all experts on brown bears from birth. And then there were the jocular quips: "I guess he was right all along. The bears really did like him! Ha! Ha!"

But even those who were against Timothy still had that Alaskan spirit of "Live and Let Live" about them. Cy at Cy's Sporting Goods told me, "The first time Treadwell came into my store, he walked over to the shotguns and I joined him in a lively conversation about bears. I made sure he knew that I thought he was nuts to try to make friends with the bears, but as long as he acted decent, he was always welcome in my store. I did find it interesting that he wanted to know why a shotgun with slugs was the choice for most Alaskans as a bear gun. I'm not saying he wanted to buy one, but he was awful interested in them. He came in several more times to look around and buy camping gear."

That one person in ten who was not against Timothy usually replied, in true Alaskan spirit, "Well, as long as he wasn't hurting anyone, I say leave the guy alone." A few others mentioned the work he did teaching children about bears. His most outspoken supporters in Kodiak are Kathleen Parker and Wanetta Ayers, who have publicly supported Timothy after getting to know him personally. Same with Willy Fulton, his pilot and friend, who told me, "He wasn't as off-the-wall as people made him out to be."

Beyond Kodiak my survey revealed a huge lack of support for Timothy Treadwell and his message of bear love. Only a smattering of people I asked throughout the country—including in his home state of California—showed support. Two people out of the seventy-eight I talked to outside of Kodiak agreed with his philosophy. A middle-aged woman in Lake Havasu City, Arizona, said, "I guess he died doing what he wanted to do," and a young woman who loves animals in Boise, Idaho, told me, "I liked that Timothy Treadwell had bridged the gap between humans and wild animals."

Timothy Treadwell's support is found not in any specific geographic locale but among the memberships of conservation organizations such as the Sierra Club, Audubon Society, and Sea Shepherd Conservation Society. But the real core of Treadwell support is centered among the animal rights and eco-warrior groups clustered in the Malibu, California, area. Their Web sites posted eulogies for Treadwell that evoked knighthood and sainthood and referred to Timothy as a visionary, a fearless protector not only of the grizzly bear but of all wild animals.

These eulogies are long and too numerous to include here, but two stand out and warrant attention. Captain Paul Watson of Sea Shepherd, who enlisted Timothy to protest the killing of harp seals in Canada, wrote a long, flowery eulogy and ended it with a quote from another conservationist, former president Teddy Roosevelt, an ironic choice since Roosevelt was an avid big-game hunter who killed several grizzlies for the walls of his trophy room.

Louisa Wilcox, formerly of the Sierra Club and now Wild Bears Project Director for the Natural Resources Defense Council, wrote a eulogy that appeared on the Grizzly People Web site and captures the emotion and philosophy of the typical Treadwell supporter. (Timothy named one of his bears in honor of Louisa.) Louisa wrote, in part: *No one who has seen Timothy's photos and films, or heard him speak did not, for a moment, reflect upon wild nature afresh, deeply, personally, and with a renewed energy to defend it. Looking at his images was as if seeing into the soul of a bear. Watching him perform in a classroom, you saw a magician who explained the mysteries of bears and their lives in such a way that children emerged glowing, as if they too were the discoverers of wild America. Hearing him talk about his bears, by name, with their bonds of affection, quirky behavior, and playful antics, you felt that you were let in on great secrets that few receive today—or have forgotten as wilderness has been paved over and subdivided. In an interview with David Letterman, you saw a quick wit, returning each Letterman volley with panache, sparkle, and a hint of an Australian accent. In a filmed sequence of Timothy singing to a mother bear, flat on her back, with two cubs nursing on top of her, you imagined for a moment that she too enjoyed the song of gentleness. And you had no doubt that you were hearing a "Bear Whisperer."*

Respected bear biologists may adamantly disagree with Louisa Wilcox's grandiose eulogy of Timothy Treadwell, but they can sympathize with the Louisa Wilcoxes of the world. She and others like her lost a champion of their cause—a leader of the current eco-warrior movement who was rapidly gaining national recognition. Biologist Tom Smith also liked Timothy Treadwell the human being—a lot. But what he never liked was Timothy Treadwell, the bear whisperer.

"I am truly sorry about Timothy's death," Tom states emphatically, "and I don't want to disrespect the memory of a dead man, but I've read his book twice, and I found nothing useful in it, nothing that was not already known. The guy was in Katmai for thirteen years, and he never produced a single document or insight that would help the plight of the bear. Show me one thing that Timothy produced from his book, from his videos, from his talks that would help the bears.

"I'm sorry. I don't want to sound harsh, but Timothy did more harm to the bears than good. He habituated many bears in his drive to get close to them to prove to the world that he had this clairvoyant power. And if you'll sit back and take a close look at the videos of him getting close to the bears, it becomes obvious that he was doing little more than harassing them. They didn't want him there beside them; they just put up with him because they didn't know what else to do with this human who kept getting in their faces.

"I've thought long and hard about Timothy, and why he was always out there, and I've concluded that there simply had to be something wrong with the guy. The entire world of bear biologists tell him there's no more poaching, but he insists he's there to stop poachers. They tell him there's no reason to be out there harassing the bears, and he says he's doing research, but when you press him about his research, he lopes off like a bear! I think he was mentally unstable, and somehow the Hollywood crowd picked up on it and decided he was a genius."

Biologist Sterling Miller, who fifteen years earlier had tagged the big red bear that was killed at the site of the tragedy, is more to the point: "Everybody who is knowledgeable about bears has long had concerns about Timothy Treadwell and the message he was giving to the public. I think he showed up on the Katmai Coast with an agenda, and he filtered all his bear experiences through it to fit that agenda.

"His biggest reason for being there was to protect the bears from poachers. I'm still hearing that even today, but bear biologists who have spent twice as much time in that area than Timothy have said over and over that there is no poaching going on, and hasn't been for a long time. Take the poaching claim away, and anyone who is a Treadwell advocate has got to look in the mirror and ask themselves why Timothy Treadwell continued to make such a claim when all the evidence proved otherwise. I think there were other reasons for Timothy being at Katmai year after year, and they didn't have anything to do with bears. I think they had more to do with self-recognition and self-aggrandizing."

Chris Servheen, grizzly bear recovery coordinator for the U.S. Fish and Wildlife Service in the northern Rocky Mountains, wrings his hands over the Treadwell episode. "We have two people dead, and two bears dead," he says, "and now this message has been sent all over the country that bears kill people, and that's the real tragedy here.

"People shouldn't see this incident as representative of the behavior of wild bears. This whole thing could have been avoided. Now, we have people who are unreasonably afraid of bears, who don't know the whole story. We work so hard to get a good message out to people, but it can be completely negated by something like this.

"Now we have to start all over with the message that grizzly bears are wild animals. They are not gentle creatures much like a human being. They need to be treated and respected as wild animals. We need to give them the space they need to go about their lives in the wild."

Chuck Jonkel, who's been studying bears for several decades and now heads the Great Bear Foundation, has had it with the Timothy Treadwell bear-whisperer types. "I think the guy was in it for the recognition and the money. Anyone who truly cares about bears would not push his warped ideas on these animals. It's a fact that these 'up-close-and-personal' encounters condition a bear and cause behavioral changes. What these people are really doing is stressing the bear out to the point that it quits acting wild. What kind of a legacy is that?"

I personally like Louisa Wilcox's eulogy of Timothy Treadwell. However, there is a huge difference between a eulogy and legacy. A eulogy is a feel-good word of praise for a dead person by his friends, while a legacy is the totality of what that person has passed on to the rest of the world. And therein lies the contradiction that is Timothy Treadwell's life.

Timothy Treadwell's stated purpose for being at Katmai was to learn the secret life of the brown grizzly bear and to protect it from poachers. Yet a plethora of wildlife biologists have stated that in thirteen years Timothy produced nothing of scientific merit. Nothing. And most certainly his vigilance in warding off supposed poachers is something better left to a psychologist to address. But let's face it, none of us are perfect, either. Lots of flawed humans have aspired to a higher calling and achieved it despite their personal shortcomings.

Timothy Treadwell's shortcomings, I believe, include his much-stated aversion to pain-causing defense tools such as bear spray and electric fences. He had especially chided wildlife biologists about their use of electric fences, calling them cowards who had no place in the wilderness if they were so afraid of the bears that they had to resort to pain to feel safe. But Timothy had used bear spray to ward off an attacking subadult he'd obviously misnamed Cupcake, and he'd also used—or attempted to use—an electric fence at one point to ward off prowling bears at night.

Despite Timothy's failings, the selfless giving of his time and effort to educate such an enormous number of children annually about bear behavior is laudable. But like everything else in Timothy Treadwell's life, even the simple task of sharing his love for the bear with children has become cloaked in doubt and suspicion.

"I watched a video of Tim speaking to fourth graders about bears," biologist Tom Smith mentions. "The guy was animated and had all the kids laughing, but his talk was peppered with biological inaccuracies. I wonder if he ever bothered to inform those schools, or the teachers, or those kids that most of what he was showing on film had been done illegally, that he was moving within mere feet of those bears in violation of national park rules. What kind of a message is that to send to children? And now that he's dead, what kind of a message is his death sending to those kids who heard from Tim about how cuddly and cute brown bears are?"

A document about Treadwell circulating on the Internet posed other questions on this subject. If Timothy's presentations reached

10,000 kids every year, with the average class size being about thirty kids, that would mean he'd have to give at least 330 presentations annually. Where did he find the time for that many presentations, even if he addressed multiple classes at once? After all, he was spending five months each year in Alaska, then a month or so in Canada protesting the harp seal harvest.

Anyone who has a hard time swallowing Tim's figure of reaching 10,000 kids annually will choke on this next tidbit. In a letter dated April 2, 2002, and addressed to Katmai superintendent Deb Liggett, he wrote: "I've enclosed a few more letters from children who learned much from my charity education programs. This year I will reach at least 15,000 kids."

Timothy had methodically designed his own legacy, complete with hyperbolic descriptions of his metaphysical bear whispering and his quixotic existence as the savior and protector of defenseless half-ton beasts. But as Timothy's own friend Alan Sanders said with sadness after Tim's death, "He tried to write his own legacy, but it doesn't work that way. You can't control how people think about you after you die."

If it is left to the living to decide, what then is Timothy Treadwell's legacy and to whom will it be passed on? If Timothy wasn't who he said he was, and if he didn't protect the bears from poachers (or even save two from himself), and if his message to schoolchildren is suspect and riddled with illegal activities, how then shall the world ultimately view Timothy Treadwell?

Biologist Sterling Miller told me he considered Timothy a charlatan, which surprised me because Sterling is normally a mild-mannered, considerate man. But Miller's appraisal might be the kindest of all. *Webster's New Ideal Dictionary* definition of a charlatan is a person who pretends to have knowledge or ability he does not have. In Timothy's case, to think that he was anything but a charlatan would be to imply instead that he was calculating, conniving, devious, deceitful, misleading, and other less benign adjectives.

Timothy Treadwell's supporters can still fashion a respectable legacy for their hero, but their goals must become realistic and transcend the initial, understandable phase of tearful eulogies. It's time for his supporters to put the ghost poachers to rest and produce something tangible, such as a bear conservation program that actually helps bears.

Unfortunately, that hasn't been the case so far. The 2004 Mountainfilm Telluride Festival in Colorado featured a "Remembering Timothy Treadwell" segment in their schedule of programs. After a visual tribute, during which dry eyes were scarce, a panel convened and addressed these questions: "Must a person be credited [as a degreed wildlife biologist] for his contributions to be accepted in the scientific world? Should Treadwell be held to a different standard of responsibility for his death than any other outdoor enthusiast? Where is the line drawn on an activist's ability to define his own mission?"

A panel discussion usually encompasses a good mix of all concerned parties, but this panel consisted of Jewel Palovak, Treadwell's best friend and Grizzly People Coordinator; Louisa Wilcox, a personal friend and author of the "Bear Whisperer" eulogy; and Captain Paul Watson of Sea Shepherd Conservation Society, another Treadwell supporter. Not a single official from the State of Alaska's Fish and Game Department was in attendance, nor were any recognized bear biologists. Neither were any laypersons with proven expertise in this area, such as Chuck Bartlebaugh of the Center for Wildlife Information.

Timothy's supporters might now consider this suggestion: How about developing a realistic (meaning less emotion and hype and more tangible results) bear-friendly and tourist-friendly program at Hallo Bay in Katmai? And furnishing the approximately $30,000 needed annually for the salaries of two seasonal park rangers to monitor activity there? How about lobbying for a 200-yard minimum bear-viewing limit to allow the bears some breathing room. The place is overrun with tourists and bear-viewing planes coming at the beleaguered bears from all directions. I personally watched planes circling low over stressed-out bears feeding in the sedge grass fields. I saw planes flying just a hundred feet over other bears migrating to the clam flats during low tide. A program to alleviate danger for both animals and humans and to ensure that life goes on as it should in the Grizzly Sanctuary could be the beginning of a positive legacy for Timothy Treadwell.

Author's Note

THE DESIRE TO WRITE THIS BOOK consumed me from the moment I heard about Timothy Treadwell's death. I was not interested in capitalizing on another human being's misfortune; rather, I wanted to correct an error in judgement I'd committed four years earlier.

Back in 2000 I wrote a book about bear attacks and how to avoid them. In the conclusion of the book, I used Timothy's rash behavior among brown grizzly bears as an example of how not to act around bears. To my surprise the editor felt I was being too personal and critical, and he strongly suggested I take out the Treadwell section. After much debate I took the safe path and removed any mention of Timothy Treadwell. I doubt that seeing my criticisms would have dissuaded him from his behavior any more than the warnings of Roland Dixon and the good people at Katmai National Park did. However, I ought not to have kept silent. More than one person might have been helped by reading that information.

While writing this book I had several challenges to overcome. My biggest challenge was gaining access to people who knew Timothy and Amie and could provide answers that would help the reader understand why their lives ended so horribly at Alaska's Katmai National Park in that rain-swept alder thicket Timothy called the Grizzly Maze. Some family and friends, such as Jewel Palovak and Louisa Wilcox, refused my inquiries. Others, such as Carol Dexter (Tim's mother) and Roland Dixon (Tim's chief financial supporter), were magnanimous in their assistance—furnishing information about Timothy that gave a more complete picture of this very complex person.

My biggest failure in gaining access to sources was with Willie Fulton, the floatplane pilot who arrived the morning of October 6, 2003, to pick up Tim and Amie, and almost lost his life when the big red bear found at the campsite chased him back to the plane. As Timothy's pilot and confidant, I felt that Willie could furnish vital information about Tim's final days. I approached Willie on the dock at Kodiak Island,

Alaska, on June 21, 2004, and waited while he posed for a picture with four bear-viewing clients he'd just brought back from Katmai. After introducing myself I told Willie that I was writing a book about Timothy and asked if we could discuss the events of Timothy's death. "Sure," Willie agreed with a friendly shrug. "Call me tonight and we'll set up a time to meet over coffee and talk." We exchanged phone numbers. But that night Willie phoned me. "Listen," he said abruptly, "I don't want to talk." I understand his reticence. I'm sorry not to have his perspective reflected more fully in this book.

I'm also sorry not to have been able to include a photo of Amie Huguenard in the book. Because Amie is an important if often over-looked part of the Timothy Treadwell story, I attempted to secure a usable photo. I was unsuccessful. Curious readers can search online for the various Associated Press news reports that appeared at the time of Amie's death, which include a family photo of her.

Another challenge was to weed through all the misinformation and hype surrounding Tim and Amie, and furnish readers with an accurate account of their lives and tragic deaths. For example, most magazine articles in the weeks immediately following the tragedy did not get the day of their deaths correct, claiming they were killed on Sunday, October 6, 2003. However, the time-coded audio tape that recorded the agonizing sounds of their deaths places the time of the attack from 1:47 to 1:53 P.M. (6 minutes, 21 seconds) on October 5, 2003.

I gleaned many of the details I've used in this book from a two-inch-thick stack of reports dealing with Timothy Treadwell that was sent to me by officials at Katmai National Park under the Freedom of Information Act. For example, it was while poring through these papers that I discovered the existence of an electric fence that Tim had surreptitiously used at one time or another, contrary to his publicly stated abhorrence of them as instruments of cruelty to bears and foxes.

The one void that remained was what exactly occurred in the days and hours leading up to Amie and Tim's deaths. Tim and Amie did leave the Grizzly Maze, only to return three days later. Treadwell's diary does mention that he and Amie had been arguing about his getting too close to the bears, and a video clip does show Amie looking frightened and leaning away from a passing bear. Tim's diary does mention that the bears were very testy and fighting among themselves because the late salmon run had failed. From this information I pieced together a probable scenario of the aggressiveness of the bears during hyperphasia (the phase in which they concentrate on consuming vast amounts of calories directly before hibernation) that Tim and Amie might have witnessed. And, as is now widely known, the final six minutes of Tim and Amie's lives were recorded in horrific detail by Tim's camera's audio tape, although the lens cap was still in place.

Several early articles on Timothy's death mentioned that Tim had an argument with an airline ticket agent at Kodiak, leading to the cancellation of his and Amie's planned auto tour of Denali National Park. According to these articles, it was this argument that ultimately sent them back to the Grizzly Maze. The source for this information came from an *Anchorage Daily News* article in which Alaska state trooper Sgt. Maurice Hughes is reported to have found information in Treadwell's journal alluding to a problem with a ticket agent. Hughes is quoted as saying, "He cancelled a driving trip around Alaska with Huguenard because he became angry with an airline employee about the cost of a change fee for their flight from Kodiak." However, I found no evidence to support this contention. I spent two hours interviewing agents at Kodiak's tiny airport but could find no one, including the manager, who recalled such an incident. My guess is that this problem with an airline ticketing agent may have arisen on a connecting flight at another airport.

Most investigators believe the big red bear killed Amie and Tim. I disagree. A half-ton brute like that big red bear would have killed Timothy in a matter of seconds, yet the audio records a prolonged attack approaching seven minutes, which indicates to me that they were most likely killed by a much smaller bear—the 300-pound subadult bear found near the site by investigators—that then fled when the big red bear arrived.

Any dead animal, be it a bear or human, becomes carrion and a coveted food source for a bear. This explains why the big red bear chased Willy Fulton back to his floatplane, and why the same bear charged the approaching rangers. Any bear guarding its food cache would have acted as aggressively. The subadult bear who later stalked the rangers is the one that exhibited the classic predatory action of a bear purposefully approaching humans.

I have endeavoured to be diligent in my attention to detail and accuracy while writing this book. Any omissions or errors on my part are unintentional. Lastly, I would like to explain that I have dedicated the book to the memory of Timothy and Amie as an act of respect and acknowledgment for the worthiness of these two lost lives.

Recommended Reading

Brown, Gary. *Outwitting Bears.* Guilford, Connecticut: The Lyons Press, 2001.

Craighead, Frank C. *The Track of the Grizzly.* Sierra Club Books, 1982.

Herrero, Stephen. *Bear Attacks: Their Causes and Avoidance.* Guilford, Connecticut: The Lyons Press, 2002.

Lapinski, Mike. *Self Defense for Nature Lovers.* Stevensville, Montana: Stoneydale Press, 1998.

_____. *True Stories of Bear Attacks: Who Survived and Why— A Case for Bear Pepper Spray.* Portland, Oregon: Westwinds Press, 2004.

McMillion, Scott. *Mark of the Grizzly: True Stories of Recent Bear Attacks and the Hard Lessons Learned.* Guilford, Connecticut: Falcon Publishing, 1998.

McNamee, Thomas. *The Grizzly Bear.* New York: Alfred A. Knopf, 1985.

Olson, Jack. *Night of the Grizzlies.* New York: Putnam Books, 1996.

Russell, Andy. *Grizzly Country.* Guilford, Connecticut: The Lyons Press, 2000.

Schneider, Bill. *Where the Grizzly Walks: The Future of the Great Bear.* Guilford, Connecticut: Falcon Press, 2003.

Stringhamn, Stephen. *Beauty Within the Beast.* Santa Ana, California: Seven Locks Press, 2002.

Treadwell, Timothy, and Jewel Palovak. *Among Grizzlies: Living with Wild Bears in Alaska.* New York: HarperCollins Publishers, 1997.

Walker, Tom. *The Way of the Grizzly: The Bears of Alaska's Famed McNeil River.* Stillwater, Minnesota: Voyageur Press, 1998.

Sources

Ayers, Wanetta. "Timothy Treadwell Faced His Greatest Fears." *Anchorage Press.*

Brother Bear. Aaron Blaise and Robert Walker, Directors. Walt Disney. 2003.

Bennett, Joel. "Treadwell Cared for the Future of Bears." *Anchorage Daily News* October 16, 2003.

Corwin, Jeff. *Going Wild with Jeff Corwin.* The Disney Channel. 1997-1999.

Dateline NBC. MSNBC. 1998.

The David Letterman Show. CBS Broadcasting Inc. 2001.

Devlin, Sherry. "Mauled Filmmaker Was Warned About His Behavior." *Missoulian.* October 12, 2003.

D'Ore, Rachel. "Tape Captures Fatal Bear Attack." *Missoulian.* October 10, 2003.

Grizzlies Among the Glaciers. Wildwatch Productions, 2002.

Grizzly People. http:// www.grizzlypeople.com.

Hittell, Theodore H. *The Adventures of James Casper Adams, Mountaineer and Grizzly Bear Hunter of California.* 1861.

Hyman, Steve and Jia-Rui Chang. "Fearless Grizzly Activist Tempted Fate and Lost." *Los Angeles Times.* October 13, 2003.

Interagency Grizzly Bear Commission. Various documents.

Jans, Nick. "Timothy Treadwell's Fatal Obsession." *Alaska Magazine.* February 2004.

Jerome, Richard. "A Sad and Grizzly End." *People Magazine.* October 27, 2003.

Kieling, Andreas. *Mutual of Omaha's Grizzly Encounters.* Animal Planet. 2004.

Lapinski, Mike. *True Stories of Bear Attacks: Who Survived and Why.* Portland, Oregon: WestWinds Press, 2004.

The Living Desert. Walt Disney. 1953.

Medred, Craig. "Deadly Ending." *Anchorage Daily News.* March 28, 2004.

_____. "Man, Martyr, Myth." *Los Angeles Times.* December 13, 2003.

_____. "Wildlife Author Killed, Eaten by Bears He Loved," Anchorage Daily News, October 8, 2003.

Miller, Sterling. *The Man Who Loved Bears*. Audubon.

Mutual of Omaha's Wild Kingdom. 1963-1971.

"Picks and Pans." *People Magazine*. August 4, 1997.

Peacock, Doug. "Blood Brothers." *Outside Magazine-Online*. January 2004.

_____. "Outtakes News & Issues." *Hooked on the Outdoors*. April 2004.

Public Use Statistics Office, www.2.nature.nps.gov/stats/. Extensive database of National Park Service statistics. Denver, Colorado: updated November 2, 2004.

Quinn, Brian. *The Depression Sourcebook*. Lowell House, 1997.

"Remembering Timothy Treadwell." Mountainfilm Telluride Festival in Colorado. 2004.

Rennicke, Jeff. "Touched by a Grizzly." *Backpacker*. May 2003.

Revenko, Igor. "In Memory of Vitaly Nickolaenko." *International Bear News*. February 2004.

Russell, Charlie. *Spirit Bear: Encounters with the White Bear of the Western Rain Forest*. Toronto: Key Porter Books: 1999.

Stouffer, Marty. *Wild America*. PBS.

Storer, Tracy and Lloyd Trevis Jr. *California Grizzly*. Berkeley: University of California Press, 1995.

Timothy Treadwell Correspondence and Incident Packet from Katmai National Park, released under the Freedom of Information Act.

Treadwell, Timothy and Jewel Palovak. *Among Grizzlies: Living with Wild Bears in Alaska*. New York: HarperCollins Publishers, 1997.

Treadwell, Timothy. *Grizzly Diaries*. The Discovery Channel.

_____. Letter to Roland Dixon, September 14, 2003. "Some Bet on My Death," *Outside Magazine*. January 2004.

The Tom Snyder Show. CBS. 1998.

Turner, Jeff. Grizzly: *Face to Face*. British Broadcasting Company. 2001.

Wallace, David. "Activist Died Doing What He Loved." *Malibu Times.* February 13, 2004.

Zeman, Ned. "The Man Who Loved Grizzlies." *Vanity Fair Magazine.* May 2004.

In addition, from March through October 2004, during the researching and writing of this book, I conducted interviews with the following experts: Angus Brown, Chuck Bartlebaugh, Deb Liggett, Dr. Charles Jonkel, George Neyssen, Sterling Miller, Terry Smith, and Tom Smith.

About the Author

MIKE LAPINSKI is the author of eleven outdoor and nature books and hundreds of magazine articles. His photos have appeared as inside and cover art in a variety of magazines and books. Mike is considered an expert on the use of bear pepper spray and often speaks on this subject, as well as on bears and self-defense for nature lovers. Mike lives with his wife, Aggie, most of the year in Superior, Montana, close to grizzlies and grizzly country. While the bears are hibernating, Mike and Aggie live in Lake Havasu City, Arizona, where Mike writes about jaguars and ocelots and other wilderness animals of the Southwest.